# Simply Gratitude & Daily Wins

- A 90 DAY JOURNAL -

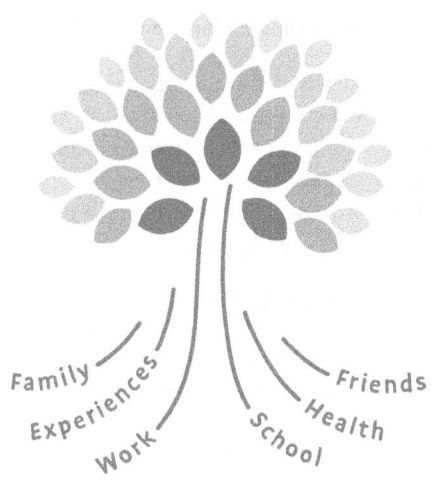

Mary Parrish

**Copyright, © Mary Parrish 2023**

All rights reserved. No part of this book may be reproduced in any form or by any electronic or mechanical means, including information storage and retrieval systems, without permission in writing from the author and copyright holder, except in the case of brief quotations embodied in critical articles and reviews. The moral rights of the author have been asserted.

Paperback ISBN: 978-1-7392604-6-0

For more information please visit www.simply-well-being.com.

# Contents

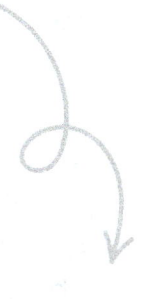

Welcome  *4*

**Daily Gratitude Journal**  *11–117*

**Daily Wins Journal**  *170–120*

Acknowledgements  *173*

About the Author  *175*

# Welcome

Welcome to my Simply Gratitude and Daily Wins journal. This daily journal goes hand-in-hand with my personal development book Simply Well-Being, where I show you how to transform your overall well-being using simple, practical activities and exercises which you can incorporate into your daily living. Simply Well-Being discusses all aspects of your well-being (the mental, physical and spiritual) and demonstrates how you need to focus on all three aspects in order to experience overall wellness.

Two very important exercises which I talk about are daily gratitude and daily wins. This journal will allow you to experience for yourself the benefits of thinking about and recording your daily appreciations and successes. I hope that you will commit to completing 30 days and then 60 days and then 90 days, so that you fully experience the positive effects these simple exercises can have on your life. Thank you for choosing this 90 day journal.

## Why is an 'Attitude of Gratitude' beneficial?

Having an attitude of gratitude really can transform your life in a matter of weeks. Regardless of how you currently feel or where you are in your life right now, by practising gratitude and appreciating all of the good in your life, you can begin to manifest and experience more of what you want. Try for yourself for 30 days and see the results.

## Why does this work?

Like attracts like. What you think about you bring about. The law of attraction is one of the most powerful universal laws, which states that you will attract into your life that which you focus upon. Once you understand how the law of attraction works, you can start to change things you want to change and attract whatever you desire into your life. By focusing on being grateful and appreciating things around you, you are basically saying to the universe 'Thank you so much, I'd like some more of this please'.

Expressing gratitude acts like a magnet for more positivity and there is always something to be grateful for. Writing down and recording what you feel grateful for each day has a number of positive psychological benefits. You can feel calmer, brighter, more confident, stronger, more positive and ultimately happier as a result.

Gratitude serves as a powerful tool to shift your focus towards the positive aspects of your life, generating a sense of contentment and fulfillment. By consciously practising gratitude you acknowledge all the blessings, big or small, that you may often take for granted.

But don't take my word for it. Use this journal to try this simple practise for a few weeks and then review how it makes you feel.

It's a good idea to do this exercise just before bedtime. Thinking positive thoughts before you sleep not only improves your sleep but also ensures that you awake on a positive vibration too.

Write down three to five things which you are most grateful for that day. Try and make them different from yesterday. Some topics to get you started could include events or experiences which have happened today, family, friends, colleagues, your home, where you live, food, water, possessions you own, your environment, the weather, money, your health etc. The topics are endless once you get thinking.

Examples to get you started:

- I am grateful for all the food which nourished my body today
- I am grateful for always having access to clean running water
- I am grateful for my Mum who is always there to listen
- I am grateful for my friend 'name' who encouraged me today
- I am grateful for my health and for feeling great today
- I am grateful for my room and having my own space
- I am grateful for my new Nike trainers which make me feel good
- I am grateful for the sunshine today which made me smile

Hopefully you get the idea and once you get started more and more things will come to mind which you are thankful for.

## Why is recording our Daily Wins a good idea?

As well as recording aspects which you are appreciating each day, another beneficial daily exercise is to record your daily wins.

Put simply, seeing your achievements written down on paper helps to boost both your self-esteem and your self-confidence. No matter how big or small your accomplishments are, writing them down gives you the opportunity to see all the positive aspects in your life and the wonderful progress which you are making daily.

It is all too easy to get overwhelmed with everything which you have to do each day. When you feel like there isn't enough time or that you're not making as much progress as you think you should, you can feel less than positive about yourself. The reality is that you are amazing, you are doing an awesome job and you are achieving far more each and every day than you give yourself credit for. Reviewing your daily wins provides tangible evidence of your progress and can remind you of all the obstacles which you have overcome as well as acting as an invaluable source of motivation. This simple exercise of writing down your achievements at the end of each day will demonstrate to you quickly that you are extremely effective. It is all about taking small steps daily and congratulating yourself on a job well done.

Aspects to think about when considering your daily wins are, first of all what you have accomplished or completed today and secondly, how you felt emotionally and physically. Feeling positive, happy or emotionally balanced during the day is a huge win.

Every day in this journal there is also a chance to give each aspect of your well-being a score out of ten. This in turn will help you to think about what you want to achieve tomorrow and how you want to feel and be.

Examples to get you started :

- Ate three healthy meals
- Played football / netball / sport of choice
- Walked the dog
- Completed specific assignment / work project / meeting
- Helped a friend with...
- Went shopping
- Felt positive for most of the day
- Enjoyed spending time with...

The simple practise of recording and appreciating your daily wins helps to develop a positive mindset, boosts your sense of confidence and enhances your motivation. This is extremely beneficial for your well-being, future growth and success.

## How to use this journal.

Each evening before sleep, take 3–5 minutes of time to fill in your gratitude diary. Think about and write down what you are grateful for today, what made you smile or feel happy and then think about the one thing which you are most grateful for.

There is a positive affirmation at the bottom of each page for you to read and say out loud to yourself. I recommend that you repeat it at least three times.

Once you have completed this, turn to the back of the journal and think about and write down your wins for the day. You can also give each aspect of your well-being a score out of ten in terms of how you felt today.

After 30, 60 and 90 days there is a review page so that you can celebrate your success and assess how you are feeling about the exercises. If you miss a day, don't beat yourself up, just start again tomorrow. It's all good.

Have fun!

www.simply-well-being.com

A GRATEFUL HEART IS A MAGNET FOR MIRACLES

# Daily Gratitude Journal

# DAILY GRATITUDE

DATE ___/___/___

**TODAY I AM GRATEFUL FOR**

..................................................................................
..................................................................................
..................................................................................
..................................................................................
..................................................................................
..................................................................................
..................................................................................

**WHAT MADE ME FEEL HAPPY TODAY?**

~~~~~~~~~~~~~~~~~~~~~~~~~~~~~~~~~~~~~~~~~~~~~~~~~
~~~~~~~~~~~~~~~~~~~~~~~~~~~~~~~~~~~~~~~~~~~~~~~~~
~~~~~~~~~~~~~~~~~~~~~~~~~~~~~~~~~~~~~~~~~~~~~~~~~

**THE ONE THING WHICH I AM MOST GRATEFUL FOR TODAY IS**

----------------------------------------------------------------
----------------------------------------------------------------

**TODAY'S AFFIRMATION:** I am enough

# DAILY GRATITUDE

DATE ___ / ___ / ___

**TODAY I AM GRATEFUL FOR**

.................................................................
.................................................................
.................................................................
.................................................................
.................................................................
.................................................................
.................................................................

**WHAT MADE ME FEEL HAPPY TODAY?**

**THE ONE THING WHICH I AM MOST GRATEFUL FOR TODAY IS**

**TODAY'S AFFIRMATION:**

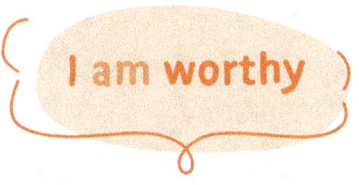

I am worthy

# DAILY GRATITUDE

DATE ___ / ___ / ___

**TODAY I AM GRATEFUL FOR**

..................................................................................
..................................................................................
..................................................................................
..................................................................................
..................................................................................
..................................................................................
..................................................................................

**WHAT MADE ME FEEL HAPPY TODAY?**

~~~~~~~~~~~~~~~~~~~~~~~~~~~~~~~~~~~~~~~~~~~~~~~~~~~~~~~~~~~~~~~~~~~~~~~~~~~~~~~~~~
~~~~~~~~~~~~~~~~~~~~~~~~~~~~~~~~~~~~~~~~~~~~~~~~~~~~~~~~~~~~~~~~~~~~~~~~~~~~~~~~~~
~~~~~~~~~~~~~~~~~~~~~~~~~~~~~~~~~~~~~~~~~~~~~~~~~~~~~~~~~~~~~~~~~~~~~~~~~~~~~~~~~~

**THE ONE THING WHICH I AM MOST GRATEFUL FOR TODAY IS**

----------------------------------------------------------------------------------
----------------------------------------------------------------------------------

**TODAY'S AFFIRMATION:** I am happy & healthy

# DAILY GRATITUDE

DATE ___/___/___

### TODAY I AM GRATEFUL FOR

................................................................
................................................................
................................................................
................................................................
................................................................
................................................................
................................................................

### WHAT MADE ME FEEL HAPPY TODAY?

~~~~~~~~~~~~~~~~~~~~~~~~~~~~~~~~~~~~~~~~~~~~~~~~~~~~~~~~~~~~~~~~
~~~~~~~~~~~~~~~~~~~~~~~~~~~~~~~~~~~~~~~~~~~~~~~~~~~~~~~~~~~~~~~~
~~~~~~~~~~~~~~~~~~~~~~~~~~~~~~~~~~~~~~~~~~~~~~~~~~~~~~~~~~~~~~~~

### THE ONE THING WHICH I AM MOST GRATEFUL FOR TODAY IS

----------------------------------------------------------------
----------------------------------------------------------------

**TODAY'S AFFIRMATION:** *Everything is possible*

# DAILY GRATITUDE

DATE ___ /___ /___

### TODAY I AM GRATEFUL FOR

..................................................................................
..................................................................................
..................................................................................
..................................................................................
..................................................................................
..................................................................................
..................................................................................

### WHAT MADE ME FEEL HAPPY TODAY?

### THE ONE THING WHICH I AM MOST GRATEFUL FOR TODAY IS

**TODAY'S AFFIRMATION:** I am awesome

# DAILY GRATITUDE

DATE ___ / ___ / ___

**TODAY I AM GRATEFUL FOR**

..................................................................
..................................................................
..................................................................
..................................................................
..................................................................
..................................................................
..................................................................

**WHAT MADE ME FEEL HAPPY TODAY?**

~~~~~~~~~~~~~~~~~~~~~~~~~~~~~~~~~~~~~~~~~~~~~~~~~~~
~~~~~~~~~~~~~~~~~~~~~~~~~~~~~~~~~~~~~~~~~~~~~~~~~~~
~~~~~~~~~~~~~~~~~~~~~~~~~~~~~~~~~~~~~~~~~~~~~~~~~~~

**THE ONE THING WHICH I AM MOST GRATEFUL FOR TODAY IS**

------------------------------------------------------------------
------------------------------------------------------------------

**TODAY'S AFFIRMATION:** I am loved

# DAILY GRATITUDE

DATE ___ / ___ / ___

### TODAY I AM GRATEFUL FOR

..........................................................................................
..........................................................................................
..........................................................................................
..........................................................................................
..........................................................................................
..........................................................................................
..........................................................................................

### WHAT MADE ME FEEL HAPPY TODAY?

~~~~~~~~~~~~~~~~~~~~~~~~~~~~~~~~~~~~~~~~~~~~~~~~~~~
~~~~~~~~~~~~~~~~~~~~~~~~~~~~~~~~~~~~~~~~~~~~~~~~~~~
~~~~~~~~~~~~~~~~~~~~~~~~~~~~~~~~~~~~~~~~~~~~~~~~~~~

### THE ONE THING WHICH I AM MOST GRATEFUL FOR TODAY IS

------------------------------------------------------------
------------------------------------------------------------

**TODAY'S AFFIRMATION:** All is well

BE YOURSELF
– EVERYONE
– ELSE IS –
ALREADY TAKEN

# DAILY GRATITUDE

DATE ___ / ___ / ___

**TODAY I AM GRATEFUL FOR**

...................................................................................
...................................................................................
...................................................................................
...................................................................................
...................................................................................
...................................................................................
...................................................................................

**WHAT MADE ME FEEL HAPPY TODAY?**

~~~~~~~~~~~~~~~~~~~~~~~~~~~~~~~~~~~~~~~~~~~~~~~~~~~~~~~~~~~~~~~~~~~~~~~~~~~~~~~~~~~
~~~~~~~~~~~~~~~~~~~~~~~~~~~~~~~~~~~~~~~~~~~~~~~~~~~~~~~~~~~~~~~~~~~~~~~~~~~~~~~~~~~
~~~~~~~~~~~~~~~~~~~~~~~~~~~~~~~~~~~~~~~~~~~~~~~~~~~~~~~~~~~~~~~~~~~~~~~~~~~~~~~~~~~

**THE ONE THING WHICH I AM MOST GRATEFUL FOR TODAY IS**

-----------------------------------------------------------------------------------
...................................................................................

**TODAY'S AFFIRMATION:**

> I am unstoppable

# DAILY GRATITUDE

DATE ___ /___ /___

**TODAY I AM GRATEFUL FOR**

.........................................................................................
.........................................................................................
.........................................................................................
.........................................................................................
.........................................................................................
.........................................................................................
.........................................................................................

**WHAT MADE ME FEEL HAPPY TODAY?**

~~~~~~~~~~~~~~~~~~~~~~~~~~~~~~~~~~~~~~~~~~~~~~~~~~~~~~~~~~~~~~~~~~~~~~~~~~~~~~~~
~~~~~~~~~~~~~~~~~~~~~~~~~~~~~~~~~~~~~~~~~~~~~~~~~~~~~~~~~~~~~~~~~~~~~~~~~~~~~~~~
~~~~~~~~~~~~~~~~~~~~~~~~~~~~~~~~~~~~~~~~~~~~~~~~~~~~~~~~~~~~~~~~~~~~~~~~~~~~~~~~

**THE ONE THING WHICH I AM MOST GRATEFUL FOR TODAY IS**

-----------------------------------------------------------------------------------
-----------------------------------------------------------------------------------

**TODAY'S AFFIRMATION:**

I manifest my dream life

# DAILY GRATITUDE

DATE ___ / ___ / ___

**TODAY I AM GRATEFUL FOR**

.................................................................................
.................................................................................
.................................................................................
.................................................................................
.................................................................................
.................................................................................
.................................................................................

**WHAT MADE ME FEEL HAPPY TODAY?**

**THE ONE THING WHICH I AM MOST GRATEFUL FOR TODAY IS**

**TODAY'S AFFIRMATION:** I love myself

# DAILY GRATITUDE

DATE ___ / ___ / ___

### TODAY I AM GRATEFUL FOR

..................................................................................
..................................................................................
..................................................................................
..................................................................................
..................................................................................
..................................................................................
..................................................................................

### WHAT MADE ME FEEL HAPPY TODAY?

~~~~~~~~~~~~~~~~~~~~~~~~~~~~~~~~~~~~~~~~~~~~~~~~~~~~~~~~~~~~~~
~~~~~~~~~~~~~~~~~~~~~~~~~~~~~~~~~~~~~~~~~~~~~~~~~~~~~~~~~~~~~~
~~~~~~~~~~~~~~~~~~~~~~~~~~~~~~~~~~~~~~~~~~~~~~~~~~~~~~~~~~~~~~

### THE ONE THING WHICH I AM MOST GRATEFUL FOR TODAY IS

------------------------------------------------------------------
------------------------------------------------------------------

**TODAY'S AFFIRMATION:** *Everything is working out for me*

# DAILY GRATITUDE

DATE ___ / ___ / ___

### TODAY I AM GRATEFUL FOR

..................................................................................
..................................................................................
..................................................................................
..................................................................................
..................................................................................
..................................................................................
..................................................................................

### WHAT MADE ME FEEL HAPPY TODAY?

~~~~~~~~~~~~~~~~~~~~~~~~~~~~~~~~~~~~~~~~~~~~~~~~~~~~~~~~~~~~~~~~
~~~~~~~~~~~~~~~~~~~~~~~~~~~~~~~~~~~~~~~~~~~~~~~~~~~~~~~~~~~~~~~~
~~~~~~~~~~~~~~~~~~~~~~~~~~~~~~~~~~~~~~~~~~~~~~~~~~~~~~~~~~~~~~~~

### THE ONE THING WHICH I AM MOST GRATEFUL FOR TODAY IS

--------------------------------------------------------------------
--------------------------------------------------------------------

**TODAY'S AFFIRMATION:**

*I am proud of myself*

# DAILY GRATITUDE

DATE ___ /___ /___

**TODAY I AM GRATEFUL FOR**

.......................................................................................
.......................................................................................
.......................................................................................
.......................................................................................
.......................................................................................
.......................................................................................
.......................................................................................

**WHAT MADE ME FEEL HAPPY TODAY?**

~~~~~~~~~~~~~~~~~~~~~~~~~~~~~~~~~~~~~~~~~~~~~~~~~~~~~~~~~~~~~~~~~~~~~~~~~~~~~~~~~~~~~~~
~~~~~~~~~~~~~~~~~~~~~~~~~~~~~~~~~~~~~~~~~~~~~~~~~~~~~~~~~~~~~~~~~~~~~~~~~~~~~~~~~~~~~~~
~~~~~~~~~~~~~~~~~~~~~~~~~~~~~~~~~~~~~~~~~~~~~~~~~~~~~~~~~~~~~~~~~~~~~~~~~~~~~~~~~~~~~~~

**THE ONE THING WHICH I AM MOST GRATEFUL FOR TODAY IS**

--------------------------------------------------------------------------------
--------------------------------------------------------------------------------

**TODAY'S AFFIRMATION:** I attract everything I want

# DAILY GRATITUDE

DATE __ /__ /__

**TODAY I AM GRATEFUL FOR**

........................................................................
........................................................................
........................................................................
........................................................................
........................................................................
........................................................................
........................................................................

**WHAT MADE ME FEEL HAPPY TODAY?**

~~~~~~~~~~~~~~~~~~~~~~~~~~~~~~~~~~~~~~~~
~~~~~~~~~~~~~~~~~~~~~~~~~~~~~~~~~~~~~~~~
~~~~~~~~~~~~~~~~~~~~~~~~~~~~~~~~~~~~~~~~

**THE ONE THING WHICH I AM MOST GRATEFUL FOR TODAY IS**

------------------------------------------------------------------------
------------------------------------------------------------------------

**TODAY'S AFFIRMATION:** *All is well*

RELAX, YOU ARE ENOUGH. BREATHE AND LET GO.

# DAILY GRATITUDE

DATE __ / __ / __

**TODAY I AM GRATEFUL FOR**

.................................................................................
.................................................................................
.................................................................................
.................................................................................
.................................................................................
.................................................................................
.................................................................................

**WHAT MADE ME FEEL HAPPY TODAY?**

~~~~~~~~~~~~~~~~~~~~~~~~~~~~~~~~~~~~~~~~~~~~~~~~~~~~~~~~~~~~~~~~~~~~~~~~~~~~~~~~~
~~~~~~~~~~~~~~~~~~~~~~~~~~~~~~~~~~~~~~~~~~~~~~~~~~~~~~~~~~~~~~~~~~~~~~~~~~~~~~~~~
~~~~~~~~~~~~~~~~~~~~~~~~~~~~~~~~~~~~~~~~~~~~~~~~~~~~~~~~~~~~~~~~~~~~~~~~~~~~~~~~~

**THE ONE THING WHICH I AM MOST GRATEFUL FOR TODAY IS**

---------------------------------------------------------------------------------
---------------------------------------------------------------------------------

**TODAY'S AFFIRMATION:** I believe in myself

# DAILY GRATITUDE

DATE ___ /___ /___

**TODAY I AM GRATEFUL FOR**

.................................................................................
.................................................................................
.................................................................................
.................................................................................
.................................................................................
.................................................................................
.................................................................................

**WHAT MADE ME FEEL HAPPY TODAY?**

~~~~~~~~~~~~~~~~~~~~~~~~~~~~~~~~~~~~~~~~~~~~~~~~~~~~~~~~~~~~~~~~~~~~~~~~~~~~~~~~~
~~~~~~~~~~~~~~~~~~~~~~~~~~~~~~~~~~~~~~~~~~~~~~~~~~~~~~~~~~~~~~~~~~~~~~~~~~~~~~~~~
~~~~~~~~~~~~~~~~~~~~~~~~~~~~~~~~~~~~~~~~~~~~~~~~~~~~~~~~~~~~~~~~~~~~~~~~~~~~~~~~~

**THE ONE THING WHICH I AM MOST GRATEFUL FOR TODAY IS**

---------------------------------------------------------------------------------
---------------------------------------------------------------------------------

**TODAY'S AFFIRMATION:**

I am calm and confident

# DAILY GRATITUDE

DATE ___ / ___ / ___

### TODAY I AM GRATEFUL FOR

..................................................................
..................................................................
..................................................................
..................................................................
..................................................................
..................................................................

### WHAT MADE ME FEEL HAPPY TODAY?

~~~~~~~~~~~~~~~~~~~~~~~~~~~~~~~~~~~~~~~~~~~~~~~~~~~~~~~~~~~~~~~~~~
~~~~~~~~~~~~~~~~~~~~~~~~~~~~~~~~~~~~~~~~~~~~~~~~~~~~~~~~~~~~~~~~~~
~~~~~~~~~~~~~~~~~~~~~~~~~~~~~~~~~~~~~~~~~~~~~~~~~~~~~~~~~~~~~~~~~~

### THE ONE THING WHICH I AM MOST GRATEFUL FOR TODAY IS

------------------------------------------------------------------
------------------------------------------------------------------

**TODAY'S AFFIRMATION:** I always do my best

# DAILY GRATITUDE

DATE ___ /___ /___

### TODAY I AM GRATEFUL FOR

.................................................................
.................................................................
.................................................................
.................................................................
.................................................................
.................................................................
.................................................................

### WHAT MADE ME FEEL HAPPY TODAY?

### THE ONE THING WHICH I AM MOST GRATEFUL FOR TODAY IS

**TODAY'S AFFIRMATION:** *My best is good enough*

# DAILY GRATITUDE

DATE ___ /___ /___

### TODAY I AM GRATEFUL FOR

..........................................................................................
..........................................................................................
..........................................................................................
..........................................................................................
..........................................................................................
..........................................................................................
..........................................................................................

### WHAT MADE ME FEEL HAPPY TODAY?

~~~~~~~~~~~~~~~~~~~~~~~~~~~~~~~~~~~~~~~~~~~~~~~~~~~~~~~~~~~~~~~~~~~~~~~~~~~~~~
~~~~~~~~~~~~~~~~~~~~~~~~~~~~~~~~~~~~~~~~~~~~~~~~~~~~~~~~~~~~~~~~~~~~~~~~~~~~~~
~~~~~~~~~~~~~~~~~~~~~~~~~~~~~~~~~~~~~~~~~~~~~~~~~~~~~~~~~~~~~~~~~~~~~~~~~~~~~~

### THE ONE THING WHICH I AM MOST GRATEFUL FOR TODAY IS

------------------------------------------------------------------------------
------------------------------------------------------------------------------

**TODAY'S AFFIRMATION:** *I love and approve of myself*

# DAILY GRATITUDE

DATE ___ / ___ / ___

**TODAY I AM GRATEFUL FOR**

........................................................................
........................................................................
........................................................................
........................................................................
........................................................................
........................................................................
........................................................................
........................................................................

**WHAT MADE ME FEEL HAPPY TODAY?**

~~~~~~~~~~~~~~~~~~~~~~~~~~~~~~~~~~~~~~~~
~~~~~~~~~~~~~~~~~~~~~~~~~~~~~~~~~~~~~~~~
~~~~~~~~~~~~~~~~~~~~~~~~~~~~~~~~~~~~~~~~

**THE ONE THING WHICH I AM MOST GRATEFUL FOR TODAY IS**

------------------------------------------------------------
------------------------------------------------------------

**TODAY'S AFFIRMATION:**

> I can do this

# DAILY GRATITUDE

DATE __ / __ / __

**TODAY I AM GRATEFUL FOR**

..................................................................................
..................................................................................
..................................................................................
..................................................................................
..................................................................................
..................................................................................
..................................................................................

**WHAT MADE ME FEEL HAPPY TODAY?**

~~~~~~~~~~~~~~~~~~~~~~~~~~~~~~~~~~~~~~~~~~~~~~~~~~~~~~~~~~~~~~~~~~~~~~~~~~~~~~~~~~
~~~~~~~~~~~~~~~~~~~~~~~~~~~~~~~~~~~~~~~~~~~~~~~~~~~~~~~~~~~~~~~~~~~~~~~~~~~~~~~~~~
~~~~~~~~~~~~~~~~~~~~~~~~~~~~~~~~~~~~~~~~~~~~~~~~~~~~~~~~~~~~~~~~~~~~~~~~~~~~~~~~~~

**THE ONE THING WHICH I AM MOST GRATEFUL FOR TODAY IS**

----------------------------------------------------------------------------------
----------------------------------------------------------------------------------

**TODAY'S AFFIRMATION:** All is well

BELIEVE IN
YOURSELF –
EVERYTHING
IS POSSIBLE

# DAILY GRATITUDE

DATE ___ / ___ / ___

**TODAY I AM GRATEFUL FOR**

..........................................................................
..........................................................................
..........................................................................
..........................................................................
..........................................................................
..........................................................................

**WHAT MADE ME FEEL HAPPY TODAY?**

**THE ONE THING WHICH I AM MOST GRATEFUL FOR TODAY IS**

**TODAY'S AFFIRMATION:** I can do anything

# DAILY GRATITUDE

DATE ___ /___ /___

**TODAY I AM GRATEFUL FOR**

..........................................................................
..........................................................................
..........................................................................
..........................................................................
..........................................................................
..........................................................................
..........................................................................

**WHAT MADE ME FEEL HAPPY TODAY?**

**THE ONE THING WHICH I AM MOST GRATEFUL FOR TODAY IS**

--------------------------------------------------------------------------
--------------------------------------------------------------------------

**TODAY'S AFFIRMATION:**

I make a difference

# DAILY GRATITUDE

DATE ___/___/___

### TODAY I AM GRATEFUL FOR

..................................................................
..................................................................
..................................................................
..................................................................
..................................................................
..................................................................
..................................................................

### WHAT MADE ME FEEL HAPPY TODAY?

~~~~~~~~~~~~~~~~~~~~~~~~~~~~~~~~~~~~~~~~~~~~~~~~~~~~~~~~~~~~~~~~~~
~~~~~~~~~~~~~~~~~~~~~~~~~~~~~~~~~~~~~~~~~~~~~~~~~~~~~~~~~~~~~~~~~~
~~~~~~~~~~~~~~~~~~~~~~~~~~~~~~~~~~~~~~~~~~~~~~~~~~~~~~~~~~~~~~~~~~

### THE ONE THING WHICH I AM MOST GRATEFUL FOR TODAY IS

------------------------------------------------------------------
------------------------------------------------------------------

**TODAY'S AFFIRMATION:** I am smart and strong

# DAILY GRATITUDE

DATE ___/___/___

**TODAY I AM GRATEFUL FOR**

..................................................................
..................................................................
..................................................................
..................................................................
..................................................................
..................................................................
..................................................................

**WHAT MADE ME FEEL HAPPY TODAY?**

**THE ONE THING WHICH I AM MOST GRATEFUL FOR TODAY IS**

------------------------------------------------------------------
------------------------------------------------------------------

**TODAY'S AFFIRMATION:** *I love myself just as I am*

# DAILY GRATITUDE

DATE ___ /___ /___

### TODAY I AM GRATEFUL FOR

..................................................................................
..................................................................................
..................................................................................
..................................................................................
..................................................................................
..................................................................................
..................................................................................

### WHAT MADE ME FEEL HAPPY TODAY?

~~~~~~~~~~~~~~~~~~~~~~~~~~~~~~~~~~~~~~~~~~~~~~~~~~~~~~~~~~~~~~~~~~~~
~~~~~~~~~~~~~~~~~~~~~~~~~~~~~~~~~~~~~~~~~~~~~~~~~~~~~~~~~~~~~~~~~~~~
~~~~~~~~~~~~~~~~~~~~~~~~~~~~~~~~~~~~~~~~~~~~~~~~~~~~~~~~~~~~~~~~~~~~

### THE ONE THING WHICH I AM MOST GRATEFUL FOR TODAY IS

------------------------------------------------------------------
------------------------------------------------------------------

**TODAY'S AFFIRMATION:** *I easily achieve my goals*

# DAILY GRATITUDE

DATE ___ / ___ / ___

**TODAY I AM GRATEFUL FOR**

.............................................................
.............................................................
.............................................................
.............................................................
.............................................................
.............................................................
.............................................................

**WHAT MADE ME FEEL HAPPY TODAY?**

~~~~~~~~~~~~~~~~~~~~~~~~~~~~~~~~~~~~~~~~~~~~~
~~~~~~~~~~~~~~~~~~~~~~~~~~~~~~~~~~~~~~~~~~~~~
~~~~~~~~~~~~~~~~~~~~~~~~~~~~~~~~~~~~~~~~~~~~~

**THE ONE THING WHICH I AM MOST GRATEFUL FOR TODAY IS**

-------------------------------------------------------------
-------------------------------------------------------------

**TODAY'S AFFIRMATION:**

> I am brave and courageous

# DAILY GRATITUDE

DATE ___ / ___ / ___

**TODAY I AM GRATEFUL FOR**

........................................................................
........................................................................
........................................................................
........................................................................
........................................................................
........................................................................
........................................................................

**WHAT MADE ME FEEL HAPPY TODAY?**

~~~~~~~~~~~~~~~~~~~~~~~~~~~~~~~~~~~~~~~~~~~~~~~~~~~~~~~~
~~~~~~~~~~~~~~~~~~~~~~~~~~~~~~~~~~~~~~~~~~~~~~~~~~~~~~~~
~~~~~~~~~~~~~~~~~~~~~~~~~~~~~~~~~~~~~~~~~~~~~~~~~~~~~~~~

**THE ONE THING WHICH I AM MOST GRATEFUL FOR TODAY IS**

------------------------------------------------------------
------------------------------------------------------------

**TODAY'S AFFIRMATION:** All is well

TODAY IS A *NEW DAY* –
A FRESH START

# DAILY GRATITUDE

DATE ___/___/___

**TODAY I AM GRATEFUL FOR**

..................................................................
..................................................................
..................................................................
..................................................................
..................................................................
..................................................................
..................................................................

**WHAT MADE ME FEEL HAPPY TODAY?**

~~~~~~~~~~~~~~~~~~~~~~~~~~~~~~~~~~~~~~~~~~~~~~~~~~~~~~~~~~~~~~~~~~
~~~~~~~~~~~~~~~~~~~~~~~~~~~~~~~~~~~~~~~~~~~~~~~~~~~~~~~~~~~~~~~~~~
~~~~~~~~~~~~~~~~~~~~~~~~~~~~~~~~~~~~~~~~~~~~~~~~~~~~~~~~~~~~~~~~~~

**THE ONE THING WHICH I AM MOST GRATEFUL FOR TODAY IS**

------------------------------------------------------------------
------------------------------------------------------------------

**TODAY'S AFFIRMATION:** I am enough

# DAILY GRATITUDE

DATE ___ /___ /___

**TODAY I AM GRATEFUL FOR**

........................................................................
........................................................................
........................................................................
........................................................................
........................................................................
........................................................................
........................................................................

**WHAT MADE ME FEEL HAPPY TODAY?**

**THE ONE THING WHICH I AM MOST GRATEFUL FOR TODAY IS**

------------------------------------------------------------------------
------------------------------------------------------------------------

**TODAY'S AFFIRMATION:**

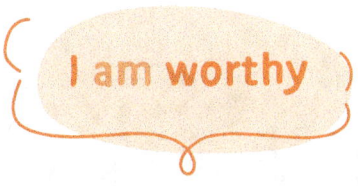

I am worthy

...you have completed 30 days!

I do hope you are enjoying the process and beginning to feel some benefits.

Take a few minutes to review the following questions:

- Are you enjoying the process of writing down your appreciations each day?
  Are you also completing your daily wins?

- Is it easier to complete now that you have been doing this for a few weeks?

- Are you feeling more positive in general?

- What other differences have you noticed if any?

- Are you ready to continue for another 30 days?

  Keep Going!

# DAILY GRATITUDE

DATE ___ / ___ / ___

### TODAY I AM GRATEFUL FOR

### WHAT MADE ME FEEL HAPPY TODAY?

### THE ONE THING WHICH I AM MOST GRATEFUL FOR TODAY IS

**TODAY'S AFFIRMATION:** I am happy & healthy

# DAILY GRATITUDE

DATE ___ /___ /___

### TODAY I AM GRATEFUL FOR

..................................................................................
..................................................................................
..................................................................................
..................................................................................
..................................................................................
..................................................................................
..................................................................................

### WHAT MADE ME FEEL HAPPY TODAY?

~~~~~~~~~~~~~~~~~~~~~~~~~~~~~~~~~~~~~~~~~~~~~~~~~~~~~~~~~~~~~~~~~~~~~~~~~~~~~~~~~~
~~~~~~~~~~~~~~~~~~~~~~~~~~~~~~~~~~~~~~~~~~~~~~~~~~~~~~~~~~~~~~~~~~~~~~~~~~~~~~~~~~
~~~~~~~~~~~~~~~~~~~~~~~~~~~~~~~~~~~~~~~~~~~~~~~~~~~~~~~~~~~~~~~~~~~~~~~~~~~~~~~~~~

### THE ONE THING WHICH I AM MOST GRATEFUL FOR TODAY IS

----------------------------------------------------------------------------------
----------------------------------------------------------------------------------

**TODAY'S AFFIRMATION:** *Everything is possible*

# DAILY GRATITUDE

DATE ___ /___ /___

### TODAY I AM GRATEFUL FOR

### WHAT MADE ME FEEL HAPPY TODAY?

### THE ONE THING WHICH I AM MOST GRATEFUL FOR TODAY IS

**TODAY'S AFFIRMATION:**

I am awesome

# DAILY GRATITUDE

DATE ___ / ___ / ___

**TODAY I AM GRATEFUL FOR**

..................................................................................
..................................................................................
..................................................................................
..................................................................................
..................................................................................
..................................................................................
..................................................................................

**WHAT MADE ME FEEL HAPPY TODAY?**

~~~~~~~~~~~~~~~~~~~~~~~~~~~~~~~~~~~~~~~~~~~~~~~~~
~~~~~~~~~~~~~~~~~~~~~~~~~~~~~~~~~~~~~~~~~~~~~~~~~
~~~~~~~~~~~~~~~~~~~~~~~~~~~~~~~~~~~~~~~~~~~~~~~~~

**THE ONE THING WHICH I AM MOST GRATEFUL FOR TODAY IS**

----------------------------------------------------------------
----------------------------------------------------------------

**TODAY'S AFFIRMATION:** I am loved

# DAILY GRATITUDE

DATE ___ /___ /___

**TODAY I AM GRATEFUL FOR**

..................................................................................
..................................................................................
..................................................................................
..................................................................................
..................................................................................
..................................................................................
..................................................................................

**WHAT MADE ME FEEL HAPPY TODAY?**

~~~~~~~~~~~~~~~~~~~~~~~~~~~~~~~~~~~~~~~~~~~~~~~~~~~~~~~~~~~~~~~~~~~~~~~~~~~~~~~~~~
~~~~~~~~~~~~~~~~~~~~~~~~~~~~~~~~~~~~~~~~~~~~~~~~~~~~~~~~~~~~~~~~~~~~~~~~~~~~~~~~~~
~~~~~~~~~~~~~~~~~~~~~~~~~~~~~~~~~~~~~~~~~~~~~~~~~~~~~~~~~~~~~~~~~~~~~~~~~~~~~~~~~~

**THE ONE THING WHICH I AM MOST GRATEFUL FOR TODAY IS**

----------------------------------------------------------------------------------
----------------------------------------------------------------------------------

**TODAY'S AFFIRMATION:** *All is well*

**DO ONE THING EVERY DAY WHICH MAKES YOU HAPPY**

# DAILY GRATITUDE

DATE ___ /___ /___

**TODAY I AM GRATEFUL FOR**

..................................................................
..................................................................
..................................................................
..................................................................
..................................................................
..................................................................
..................................................................

**WHAT MADE ME FEEL HAPPY TODAY?**

~~~~~~~~~~~~~~~~~~~~~~~~~~~~~~~~~~~~~~~~~~~~~~~~~~~~~~~~~~~~~~~~~~
~~~~~~~~~~~~~~~~~~~~~~~~~~~~~~~~~~~~~~~~~~~~~~~~~~~~~~~~~~~~~~~~~~
~~~~~~~~~~~~~~~~~~~~~~~~~~~~~~~~~~~~~~~~~~~~~~~~~~~~~~~~~~~~~~~~~~

**THE ONE THING WHICH I AM MOST GRATEFUL FOR TODAY IS**

------------------------------------------------------------------
------------------------------------------------------------------

**TODAY'S AFFIRMATION:** I am unstoppable

# DAILY GRATITUDE

DATE ___ /___ /___

### TODAY I AM GRATEFUL FOR

..............................................................................................
..............................................................................................
..............................................................................................
..............................................................................................
..............................................................................................
..............................................................................................
..............................................................................................

### WHAT MADE ME FEEL HAPPY TODAY?

### THE ONE THING WHICH I AM MOST GRATEFUL FOR TODAY IS

### TODAY'S AFFIRMATION:

**I manifest my dream life**

# DAILY GRATITUDE

DATE ___/___/___

### TODAY I AM GRATEFUL FOR

..........................................................................
..........................................................................
..........................................................................
..........................................................................
..........................................................................
..........................................................................

### WHAT MADE ME FEEL HAPPY TODAY?

### THE ONE THING WHICH I AM MOST GRATEFUL FOR TODAY IS

------------------------------------------------------------
------------------------------------------------------------

**TODAY'S AFFIRMATION:** I love myself

# DAILY GRATITUDE

DATE ___ / ___ / ___

## TODAY I AM GRATEFUL FOR

..........................................................................................
..........................................................................................
..........................................................................................
..........................................................................................
..........................................................................................
..........................................................................................
..........................................................................................

## WHAT MADE ME FEEL HAPPY TODAY?

~~~~~~~~~~~~~~~~~~~~~~~~~~~~~~~~~~~~~~~~~~~~~~~~~~~~~~~~~~~~~~~~~~~~~~~~~~~~~~~~~~~~~~~~~~~~~
~~~~~~~~~~~~~~~~~~~~~~~~~~~~~~~~~~~~~~~~~~~~~~~~~~~~~~~~~~~~~~~~~~~~~~~~~~~~~~~~~~~~~~~~~~~~~
~~~~~~~~~~~~~~~~~~~~~~~~~~~~~~~~~~~~~~~~~~~~~~~~~~~~~~~~~~~~~~~~~~~~~~~~~~~~~~~~~~~~~~~~~~~~~

## THE ONE THING WHICH I AM MOST GRATEFUL FOR TODAY IS

------------------------------------------------------------------------
------------------------------------------------------------------------

**TODAY'S AFFIRMATION:** *Everything is working out for me*

# DAILY GRATITUDE

DATE ___ / ___ / ___

**TODAY I AM GRATEFUL FOR**

..........................................................................
..........................................................................
..........................................................................
..........................................................................
..........................................................................
..........................................................................
..........................................................................

**WHAT MADE ME FEEL HAPPY TODAY?**

**THE ONE THING WHICH I AM MOST GRATEFUL FOR TODAY IS**

------------------------------------------------------
------------------------------------------------------

**TODAY'S AFFIRMATION:**

I am proud of myself

# DAILY GRATITUDE

DATE ___/___/___

**TODAY I AM GRATEFUL FOR**

.............................................................................................
.............................................................................................
.............................................................................................
.............................................................................................
.............................................................................................
.............................................................................................
.............................................................................................

**WHAT MADE ME FEEL HAPPY TODAY?**

**THE ONE THING WHICH I AM MOST GRATEFUL FOR TODAY IS**

-----------------------------------------------------------------------------
-----------------------------------------------------------------------------

**TODAY'S AFFIRMATION:**

> I attract everything I want

# DAILY GRATITUDE

DATE ___ /___ /___

### TODAY I AM GRATEFUL FOR

..................................................................
..................................................................
..................................................................
..................................................................
..................................................................
..................................................................
..................................................................

### WHAT MADE ME FEEL HAPPY TODAY?

~~~~~~~~~~~~~~~~~~~~~~~~~~~~~~~~~~~~~~~~~~~~~~~~~~~~~~~~~~~~~~~~~~
~~~~~~~~~~~~~~~~~~~~~~~~~~~~~~~~~~~~~~~~~~~~~~~~~~~~~~~~~~~~~~~~~~
~~~~~~~~~~~~~~~~~~~~~~~~~~~~~~~~~~~~~~~~~~~~~~~~~~~~~~~~~~~~~~~~~~

### THE ONE THING WHICH I AM MOST GRATEFUL FOR TODAY IS

------------------------------------------------------------------
------------------------------------------------------------------

**TODAY'S AFFIRMATION:** All is well

**BECOME**
YOUR OWN BIGGEST
AND LOUDEST
CHEERLEADER

# DAILY GRATITUDE

DATE ___/___/___

**TODAY I AM GRATEFUL FOR**

..................................................................
..................................................................
..................................................................
..................................................................
..................................................................
..................................................................
..................................................................

**WHAT MADE ME FEEL HAPPY TODAY?**

..................................................................
..................................................................
..................................................................

**THE ONE THING WHICH I AM MOST GRATEFUL FOR TODAY IS**

------------------------------------------------------------------
------------------------------------------------------------------

**TODAY'S AFFIRMATION:** I believe in myself

# DAILY GRATITUDE

DATE ___ /___ /___

**TODAY I AM GRATEFUL FOR**

..................................................................................
..................................................................................
..................................................................................
..................................................................................
..................................................................................
..................................................................................
..................................................................................

**WHAT MADE ME FEEL HAPPY TODAY?**

**THE ONE THING WHICH I AM MOST GRATEFUL FOR TODAY IS**

**TODAY'S AFFIRMATION:**

*I am calm and confident*

# DAILY GRATITUDE

DATE ___ /___ /___

**TODAY I AM GRATEFUL FOR**

.................................................................................
.................................................................................
.................................................................................
.................................................................................
.................................................................................
.................................................................................
.................................................................................

**WHAT MADE ME FEEL HAPPY TODAY?**

~~~~~~~~~~~~~~~~~~~~~~~~~~~~~~~~~~~~~~~~~~~~~~~~~
~~~~~~~~~~~~~~~~~~~~~~~~~~~~~~~~~~~~~~~~~~~~~~~~~
~~~~~~~~~~~~~~~~~~~~~~~~~~~~~~~~~~~~~~~~~~~~~~~~~

**THE ONE THING WHICH I AM MOST GRATEFUL FOR TODAY IS**

-------------------------------------------------------------------
-------------------------------------------------------------------

**TODAY'S AFFIRMATION:** I always do my best

# DAILY GRATITUDE

DATE __/__/__

### TODAY I AM GRATEFUL FOR

.................................................................................
.................................................................................
.................................................................................
.................................................................................
.................................................................................
.................................................................................
.................................................................................

### WHAT MADE ME FEEL HAPPY TODAY?

### THE ONE THING WHICH I AM MOST GRATEFUL FOR TODAY IS

- - - - - - - - - - - - - - - - - - - - - - - - - - - - - - - - - - - - - - - - -
- - - - - - - - - - - - - - - - - - - - - - - - - - - - - - - - - - - - - - - - -

**TODAY'S AFFIRMATION:** *My best is good enough*

# DAILY GRATITUDE

DATE ___ /___ /___

### TODAY I AM GRATEFUL FOR

..................................................................
..................................................................
..................................................................
..................................................................
..................................................................
..................................................................

### WHAT MADE ME FEEL HAPPY TODAY?

~~~~~~~~~~~~~~~~~~~~~~~~~~~~~~~~~~~~~~~~~~~~~~~~~~~~~~~~~~~~~~~~~~
~~~~~~~~~~~~~~~~~~~~~~~~~~~~~~~~~~~~~~~~~~~~~~~~~~~~~~~~~~~~~~~~~~
~~~~~~~~~~~~~~~~~~~~~~~~~~~~~~~~~~~~~~~~~~~~~~~~~~~~~~~~~~~~~~~~~~

### THE ONE THING WHICH I AM MOST GRATEFUL FOR TODAY IS

------------------------------------------------------------------
------------------------------------------------------------------

**TODAY'S AFFIRMATION:** *I love and approve of myself*

# DAILY GRATITUDE

DATE ___ /___ /___

**TODAY I AM GRATEFUL FOR**

................................................................................
................................................................................
................................................................................
................................................................................
................................................................................
................................................................................
................................................................................

**WHAT MADE ME FEEL HAPPY TODAY?**

~~~~~~~~~~~~~~~~~~~~~~~~~~~~~~~~~~~~~~~~~~~~~~~~~~~~~~~~~~~~~~~~~~~~~~~~~~~~~~~~
~~~~~~~~~~~~~~~~~~~~~~~~~~~~~~~~~~~~~~~~~~~~~~~~~~~~~~~~~~~~~~~~~~~~~~~~~~~~~~~~
~~~~~~~~~~~~~~~~~~~~~~~~~~~~~~~~~~~~~~~~~~~~~~~~~~~~~~~~~~~~~~~~~~~~~~~~~~~~~~~~

**THE ONE THING WHICH I AM MOST GRATEFUL FOR TODAY IS**

--------------------------------------------------------------------------------
--------------------------------------------------------------------------------

**TODAY'S AFFIRMATION:**

> I can do this

# DAILY GRATITUDE

DATE ___ /___ /___

**TODAY I AM GRATEFUL FOR**

....................................................................................
....................................................................................
....................................................................................
....................................................................................
....................................................................................
....................................................................................

**WHAT MADE ME FEEL HAPPY TODAY?**

~~~~~~~~~~~~~~~~~~~~~~~~~~~~~~~~~~~~~~~~~~~~~~~~~~~
~~~~~~~~~~~~~~~~~~~~~~~~~~~~~~~~~~~~~~~~~~~~~~~~~~~
~~~~~~~~~~~~~~~~~~~~~~~~~~~~~~~~~~~~~~~~~~~~~~~~~~~

**THE ONE THING WHICH I AM MOST GRATEFUL FOR TODAY IS**

----------------------------------------------------------------
----------------------------------------------------------------

**TODAY'S AFFIRMATION:** *All is well*

LET YOUR SMILE SHINE ALL DAY LONG – IT'S CONTAGIOUS

# DAILY GRATITUDE

DATE ___ / ___ / ___

**TODAY I AM GRATEFUL FOR**

.................................................................
.................................................................
.................................................................
.................................................................
.................................................................
.................................................................
.................................................................
.................................................................

**WHAT MADE ME FEEL HAPPY TODAY?**

~~~~~~~~~~~~~~~~~~~~~~~~~~~~~~~~~~~~~~~~~~~~~~~~~
~~~~~~~~~~~~~~~~~~~~~~~~~~~~~~~~~~~~~~~~~~~~~~~~~
~~~~~~~~~~~~~~~~~~~~~~~~~~~~~~~~~~~~~~~~~~~~~~~~~

**THE ONE THING WHICH I AM MOST GRATEFUL FOR TODAY IS**

-------------------------------------------------
-------------------------------------------------

**TODAY'S AFFIRMATION:** I can do anything

# DAILY GRATITUDE

DATE ___/___/___

### TODAY I AM GRATEFUL FOR

..................................................................
..................................................................
..................................................................
..................................................................
..................................................................
..................................................................
..................................................................

### WHAT MADE ME FEEL HAPPY TODAY?

~~~~~~~~~~~~~~~~~~~~~~~~~~~~~~~~~~~~~~~~~~~~~~~~~~~~~~~~~~~~~~~~~~
~~~~~~~~~~~~~~~~~~~~~~~~~~~~~~~~~~~~~~~~~~~~~~~~~~~~~~~~~~~~~~~~~~
~~~~~~~~~~~~~~~~~~~~~~~~~~~~~~~~~~~~~~~~~~~~~~~~~~~~~~~~~~~~~~~~~~

### THE ONE THING WHICH I AM MOST GRATEFUL FOR TODAY IS

------------------------------------------------------------------
------------------------------------------------------------------

### TODAY'S AFFIRMATION:

**I make a difference**

# DAILY GRATITUDE

DATE ___ / ___ / ___

**TODAY I AM GRATEFUL FOR**

..................................................................................
..................................................................................
..................................................................................
..................................................................................
..................................................................................
..................................................................................
..................................................................................

**WHAT MADE ME FEEL HAPPY TODAY?**

~~~~~~~~~~~~~~~~~~~~~~~~~~~~~~~~~~~~~~~~~~~~~~~~~~~~~~~~~~~~~~~~~~
~~~~~~~~~~~~~~~~~~~~~~~~~~~~~~~~~~~~~~~~~~~~~~~~~~~~~~~~~~~~~~~~~~
~~~~~~~~~~~~~~~~~~~~~~~~~~~~~~~~~~~~~~~~~~~~~~~~~~~~~~~~~~~~~~~~~~

**THE ONE THING WHICH I AM MOST GRATEFUL FOR TODAY IS**

-----------------------------------------------------------------
-----------------------------------------------------------------

**TODAY'S AFFIRMATION:** *I am smart and strong*

# DAILY GRATITUDE

DATE ___ / ___ / ___

### TODAY I AM GRATEFUL FOR

..................................................................................
..................................................................................
..................................................................................
..................................................................................
..................................................................................
..................................................................................
..................................................................................

### WHAT MADE ME FEEL HAPPY TODAY?

### THE ONE THING WHICH I AM MOST GRATEFUL FOR TODAY IS

--------------------------------------------------------------
--------------------------------------------------------------

**TODAY'S AFFIRMATION:** *I love myself just as I am*

# DAILY GRATITUDE

DATE ___ /___ /___

### TODAY I AM GRATEFUL FOR

..............................................................................
..............................................................................
..............................................................................
..............................................................................
..............................................................................
..............................................................................

### WHAT MADE ME FEEL HAPPY TODAY?

~~~~~~~~~~~~~~~~~~~~~~~~~~~~~~~~~~~~~~~~~~~~~~~~~~~~~~~~~~~~~~~~~~~~~~~~~~~~~~
~~~~~~~~~~~~~~~~~~~~~~~~~~~~~~~~~~~~~~~~~~~~~~~~~~~~~~~~~~~~~~~~~~~~~~~~~~~~~~
~~~~~~~~~~~~~~~~~~~~~~~~~~~~~~~~~~~~~~~~~~~~~~~~~~~~~~~~~~~~~~~~~~~~~~~~~~~~~~

### THE ONE THING WHICH I AM MOST GRATEFUL FOR TODAY IS

------------------------------------------------------------------------------
------------------------------------------------------------------------------

**TODAY'S AFFIRMATION:**

*I easily achieve my goals*

# DAILY GRATITUDE

DATE ___ / ___ / ___

**TODAY I AM GRATEFUL FOR**

..................................................................................
..................................................................................
..................................................................................
..................................................................................
..................................................................................
..................................................................................
..................................................................................

**WHAT MADE ME FEEL HAPPY TODAY?**

~~~~~~~~~~~~~~~~~~~~~~~~~~~~~~~~~~~~~~~~~~~~~~~~~~~~~~~~~~~~~~~~~~~~~~~~~~~~~~~~~~
~~~~~~~~~~~~~~~~~~~~~~~~~~~~~~~~~~~~~~~~~~~~~~~~~~~~~~~~~~~~~~~~~~~~~~~~~~~~~~~~~~
~~~~~~~~~~~~~~~~~~~~~~~~~~~~~~~~~~~~~~~~~~~~~~~~~~~~~~~~~~~~~~~~~~~~~~~~~~~~~~~~~~

**THE ONE THING WHICH I AM MOST GRATEFUL FOR TODAY IS**

----------------------------------------------------------------------------------
----------------------------------------------------------------------------------

**TODAY'S AFFIRMATION:** I am brave and courageous

# DAILY GRATITUDE

DATE __ / __ / __

**TODAY I AM GRATEFUL FOR**

..............................................................................
..............................................................................
..............................................................................
..............................................................................
..............................................................................
..............................................................................
..............................................................................

**WHAT MADE ME FEEL HAPPY TODAY?**

**THE ONE THING WHICH I AM MOST GRATEFUL FOR TODAY IS**

------------------------------------------------------------------------------
------------------------------------------------------------------------------

**TODAY'S AFFIRMATION:**

All is well

IT COSTS NOTHING TO
**BE A GOOD HUMAN BEING**

# DAILY GRATITUDE

DATE ___ / ___ / ___

**TODAY I AM GRATEFUL FOR**

..........................................................................................................
..........................................................................................................
..........................................................................................................
..........................................................................................................
..........................................................................................................
..........................................................................................................
..........................................................................................................

**WHAT MADE ME FEEL HAPPY TODAY?**

**THE ONE THING WHICH I AM MOST GRATEFUL FOR TODAY IS**

**TODAY'S AFFIRMATION:** I am enough

# DAILY GRATITUDE

DATE ___ / ___ / ___

**TODAY I AM GRATEFUL FOR**

..................................................................
..................................................................
..................................................................
..................................................................
..................................................................
..................................................................
..................................................................

**WHAT MADE ME FEEL HAPPY TODAY?**

**THE ONE THING WHICH I AM MOST GRATEFUL FOR TODAY IS**

**TODAY'S AFFIRMATION:**

I am worthy

# DAILY GRATITUDE

DATE ___ /___ /___

### TODAY I AM GRATEFUL FOR

..................................................................................
..................................................................................
..................................................................................
..................................................................................
..................................................................................
..................................................................................

### WHAT MADE ME FEEL HAPPY TODAY?

### THE ONE THING WHICH I AM MOST GRATEFUL FOR TODAY IS

**TODAY'S AFFIRMATION:** I am happy & healthy

# DAILY GRATITUDE

DATE __ / __ / __

### TODAY I AM GRATEFUL FOR

..................................................................................
..................................................................................
..................................................................................
..................................................................................
..................................................................................
..................................................................................
..................................................................................

### WHAT MADE ME FEEL HAPPY TODAY?

~~~~~~~~~~~~~~~~~~~~~~~~~~~~~~~~~~~~~~~~~~~~~~~~~~~~~~~~~~~~~~~~~~~~~~~~~~~~~~~~~~
~~~~~~~~~~~~~~~~~~~~~~~~~~~~~~~~~~~~~~~~~~~~~~~~~~~~~~~~~~~~~~~~~~~~~~~~~~~~~~~~~~
~~~~~~~~~~~~~~~~~~~~~~~~~~~~~~~~~~~~~~~~~~~~~~~~~~~~~~~~~~~~~~~~~~~~~~~~~~~~~~~~~~

### THE ONE THING WHICH I AM MOST GRATEFUL FOR TODAY IS

----------------------------------------------------------------------------------
----------------------------------------------------------------------------------

**TODAY'S AFFIRMATION:** *Everything is possible*

Well done on completing 60 days, you are now well on your way to creating a long-lasting positive habit.

Take a few minutes to review the following questions:

- Are you enjoying the process of writing down your appreciations each day?
- Are you finding more things to be grateful for each day?
- Are you surprised by all of your daily wins and achievements?
- Are you feeling more positive in general?
- Are you feeling calmer?
- Are you feeling happier?
- What other differences have you noticed?
- Are you ready to continue for another 30 days?

You've got this – let's go!

# DAILY GRATITUDE

DATE __ /__ /__

### TODAY I AM GRATEFUL FOR

........................................................................
........................................................................
........................................................................
........................................................................
........................................................................
........................................................................

### WHAT MADE ME FEEL HAPPY TODAY?

~~~~~~~~~~~~~~~~~~~~~~~~~~~~~~~~~~~~~~~~~~~~~~~~~~~~~~~~~~~~~~~~~~~~~~~~
~~~~~~~~~~~~~~~~~~~~~~~~~~~~~~~~~~~~~~~~~~~~~~~~~~~~~~~~~~~~~~~~~~~~~~~~
~~~~~~~~~~~~~~~~~~~~~~~~~~~~~~~~~~~~~~~~~~~~~~~~~~~~~~~~~~~~~~~~~~~~~~~~

### THE ONE THING WHICH I AM MOST GRATEFUL FOR TODAY IS

------------------------------------------------------------------------
------------------------------------------------------------------------

**TODAY'S AFFIRMATION:** *I am awesome*

# DAILY GRATITUDE

DATE ___/___/___

**TODAY I AM GRATEFUL FOR**

.................................................................................
.................................................................................
.................................................................................
.................................................................................
.................................................................................
.................................................................................
.................................................................................

**WHAT MADE ME FEEL HAPPY TODAY?**

.................................................................................
.................................................................................
.................................................................................

**THE ONE THING WHICH I AM MOST GRATEFUL FOR TODAY IS**

---------------------------------------------------------------------------------
---------------------------------------------------------------------------------

**TODAY'S AFFIRMATION:** I am loved

# DAILY GRATITUDE

DATE ___/___/___

**TODAY I AM GRATEFUL FOR**

..................................................................
..................................................................
..................................................................
..................................................................
..................................................................
..................................................................

**WHAT MADE ME FEEL HAPPY TODAY?**

~~~~~~~~~~~~~~~~~~~~~~~~~~~~~~~~~~~~~~~~~~~~~~~~~~~~~~~~~~~~~~~~~~
~~~~~~~~~~~~~~~~~~~~~~~~~~~~~~~~~~~~~~~~~~~~~~~~~~~~~~~~~~~~~~~~~~
~~~~~~~~~~~~~~~~~~~~~~~~~~~~~~~~~~~~~~~~~~~~~~~~~~~~~~~~~~~~~~~~~~

**THE ONE THING WHICH I AM MOST GRATEFUL FOR TODAY IS**

------------------------------------------------------------------
------------------------------------------------------------------

**TODAY'S AFFIRMATION:** *All is well*

THE BEST ADVICE COMES FROM YOUR GUT INSTINCT

# DAILY GRATITUDE

DATE ___/___/___

### TODAY I AM GRATEFUL FOR

..................................................................
..................................................................
..................................................................
..................................................................
..................................................................
..................................................................
..................................................................

### WHAT MADE ME FEEL HAPPY TODAY?

~~~~~~~~~~~~~~~~~~~~~~~~~~~~~~~~~~~~~~~~~~~~~~~~~~~~~~~~~~~~~~~~~~
~~~~~~~~~~~~~~~~~~~~~~~~~~~~~~~~~~~~~~~~~~~~~~~~~~~~~~~~~~~~~~~~~~
~~~~~~~~~~~~~~~~~~~~~~~~~~~~~~~~~~~~~~~~~~~~~~~~~~~~~~~~~~~~~~~~~~

### THE ONE THING WHICH I AM MOST GRATEFUL FOR TODAY IS

------------------------------------------------------------------
------------------------------------------------------------------

**TODAY'S AFFIRMATION:** I am unstoppable

# DAILY GRATITUDE

DATE ___ / ___ / ___

**TODAY I AM GRATEFUL FOR**

..................................................................................
..................................................................................
..................................................................................
..................................................................................
..................................................................................
..................................................................................
..................................................................................

**WHAT MADE ME FEEL HAPPY TODAY?**

**THE ONE THING WHICH I AM MOST GRATEFUL FOR TODAY IS**

**TODAY'S AFFIRMATION:**

I manifest my dream life

# DAILY GRATITUDE

DATE ___ /___ /___

**TODAY I AM GRATEFUL FOR**

..................................................................
..................................................................
..................................................................
..................................................................
..................................................................
..................................................................
..................................................................

**WHAT MADE ME FEEL HAPPY TODAY?**

~~~~~~~~~~~~~~~~~~~~~~~~~~~~~~~~~~~~~~~~~~~~~~~~~~~~~~~~~~~~~~~~~~
~~~~~~~~~~~~~~~~~~~~~~~~~~~~~~~~~~~~~~~~~~~~~~~~~~~~~~~~~~~~~~~~~~
~~~~~~~~~~~~~~~~~~~~~~~~~~~~~~~~~~~~~~~~~~~~~~~~~~~~~~~~~~~~~~~~~~

**THE ONE THING WHICH I AM MOST GRATEFUL FOR TODAY IS**

------------------------------------------------------------------
------------------------------------------------------------------

**TODAY'S AFFIRMATION:**

# DAILY GRATITUDE

DATE ___ /___ /___

**TODAY I AM GRATEFUL FOR**

.................................................................................
.................................................................................
.................................................................................
.................................................................................
.................................................................................
.................................................................................

**WHAT MADE ME FEEL HAPPY TODAY?**

.................................................................................
.................................................................................
.................................................................................

**THE ONE THING WHICH I AM MOST GRATEFUL FOR TODAY IS**

---------------------------------------------------------------------------------
---------------------------------------------------------------------------------

**TODAY'S AFFIRMATION:** *Everything is working out for me*

# DAILY GRATITUDE

DATE ___ / ___ / ___

### TODAY I AM GRATEFUL FOR

.................................................................................
.................................................................................
.................................................................................
.................................................................................
.................................................................................
.................................................................................
.................................................................................

### WHAT MADE ME FEEL HAPPY TODAY?

~~~~~~~~~~~~~~~~~~~~~~~~~~~~~~~~~~~~~~~~~~~~~~~~~
~~~~~~~~~~~~~~~~~~~~~~~~~~~~~~~~~~~~~~~~~~~~~~~~~
~~~~~~~~~~~~~~~~~~~~~~~~~~~~~~~~~~~~~~~~~~~~~~~~~

### THE ONE THING WHICH I AM MOST GRATEFUL FOR TODAY IS

-----------------------------------------------------------
-----------------------------------------------------------

**TODAY'S AFFIRMATION:** *I am proud of myself*

# DAILY GRATITUDE

DATE ___/___/___

**TODAY I AM GRATEFUL FOR**

..................................................................
..................................................................
..................................................................
..................................................................
..................................................................
..................................................................
..................................................................

**WHAT MADE ME FEEL HAPPY TODAY?**

**THE ONE THING WHICH I AM MOST GRATEFUL FOR TODAY IS**

**TODAY'S AFFIRMATION:** I attract everything I want

# DAILY GRATITUDE

DATE ___ / ___ / ___

**TODAY I AM GRATEFUL FOR**

..................................................................................
..................................................................................
..................................................................................
..................................................................................
..................................................................................
..................................................................................

**WHAT MADE ME FEEL HAPPY TODAY?**

~~~~~~~~~~~~~~~~~~~~~~~~~~~~~~~~~~~~~~~~~~~~~~~~~~~~
~~~~~~~~~~~~~~~~~~~~~~~~~~~~~~~~~~~~~~~~~~~~~~~~~~~~
~~~~~~~~~~~~~~~~~~~~~~~~~~~~~~~~~~~~~~~~~~~~~~~~~~~~

**THE ONE THING WHICH I AM MOST GRATEFUL FOR TODAY IS**

--------------------------------------------------------------------
--------------------------------------------------------------------

**TODAY'S AFFIRMATION:** *All is well*

**BELIEVE IN YOURSELF**
AND YOU WILL
BE UNSTOPPABLE

# DAILY GRATITUDE

DATE ___ /___ /___

**TODAY I AM GRATEFUL FOR**

..................................................................
..................................................................
..................................................................
..................................................................
..................................................................
..................................................................
..................................................................

**WHAT MADE ME FEEL HAPPY TODAY?**

..................................................................
..................................................................
..................................................................

**THE ONE THING WHICH I AM MOST GRATEFUL FOR TODAY IS**

------------------------------------------------------------------
------------------------------------------------------------------

**TODAY'S AFFIRMATION:** I believe in myself

# DAILY GRATITUDE

DATE ___ / ___ / ___

**TODAY I AM GRATEFUL FOR**

..................................................................................
..................................................................................
..................................................................................
..................................................................................
..................................................................................
..................................................................................
..................................................................................

**WHAT MADE ME FEEL HAPPY TODAY?**

**THE ONE THING WHICH I AM MOST GRATEFUL FOR TODAY IS**

------------------------------------------------------------
------------------------------------------------------------

**TODAY'S AFFIRMATION:**

I am calm and confident

# DAILY GRATITUDE

DATE ___ / ___ / ___

**TODAY I AM GRATEFUL FOR**

..................................................................................
..................................................................................
..................................................................................
..................................................................................
..................................................................................
..................................................................................
..................................................................................

**WHAT MADE ME FEEL HAPPY TODAY?**

~~~~~~~~~~~~~~~~~~~~~~~~~~~~~~~~~~~~~~~~~~~~~~~~~~~~~~~~~~~~~~~~~~~~
~~~~~~~~~~~~~~~~~~~~~~~~~~~~~~~~~~~~~~~~~~~~~~~~~~~~~~~~~~~~~~~~~~~~
~~~~~~~~~~~~~~~~~~~~~~~~~~~~~~~~~~~~~~~~~~~~~~~~~~~~~~~~~~~~~~~~~~~~

**THE ONE THING WHICH I AM MOST GRATEFUL FOR TODAY IS**

--------------------------------------------------------------------
--------------------------------------------------------------------

**TODAY'S AFFIRMATION:** I always do my best

# DAILY GRATITUDE

DATE ___ /___ /___

### TODAY I AM GRATEFUL FOR

..................................................................................
..................................................................................
..................................................................................
..................................................................................
..................................................................................
..................................................................................
..................................................................................

### WHAT MADE ME FEEL HAPPY TODAY?

### THE ONE THING WHICH I AM MOST GRATEFUL FOR TODAY IS

------------------------------------------------------------
------------------------------------------------------------

**TODAY'S AFFIRMATION:** *My best is good enough*

# DAILY GRATITUDE

DATE ___ / ___ / ___

**TODAY I AM GRATEFUL FOR**

..................................................................................
..................................................................................
..................................................................................
..................................................................................
..................................................................................
..................................................................................
..................................................................................

**WHAT MADE ME FEEL HAPPY TODAY?**

~~~~~~~~~~~~~~~~~~~~~~~~~~~~~~~~~~~~~~~~~~~~~~~~~~~~~~
~~~~~~~~~~~~~~~~~~~~~~~~~~~~~~~~~~~~~~~~~~~~~~~~~~~~~~
~~~~~~~~~~~~~~~~~~~~~~~~~~~~~~~~~~~~~~~~~~~~~~~~~~~~~~

**THE ONE THING WHICH I AM MOST GRATEFUL FOR TODAY IS**

------------------------------------------------------------
------------------------------------------------------------

**TODAY'S AFFIRMATION:**

*I love and approve of myself*

# DAILY GRATITUDE

DATE ___ / ___ / ___

**TODAY I AM GRATEFUL FOR**

......................................................................................
......................................................................................
......................................................................................
......................................................................................
......................................................................................
......................................................................................
......................................................................................
......................................................................................

**WHAT MADE ME FEEL HAPPY TODAY?**

**THE ONE THING WHICH I AM MOST GRATEFUL FOR TODAY IS**

**TODAY'S AFFIRMATION:** I can do this

# DAILY GRATITUDE

DATE ___ /___ /___

### TODAY I AM GRATEFUL FOR

..................................................................................
..................................................................................
..................................................................................
..................................................................................
..................................................................................
..................................................................................
..................................................................................

### WHAT MADE ME FEEL HAPPY TODAY?

~~~~~~~~~~~~~~~~~~~~~~~~~~~~~~~~~~~~~~~~~~~~~~~~~~~~~~~~~~~~~~~~~~
~~~~~~~~~~~~~~~~~~~~~~~~~~~~~~~~~~~~~~~~~~~~~~~~~~~~~~~~~~~~~~~~~~
~~~~~~~~~~~~~~~~~~~~~~~~~~~~~~~~~~~~~~~~~~~~~~~~~~~~~~~~~~~~~~~~~~

### THE ONE THING WHICH I AM MOST GRATEFUL FOR TODAY IS

----------------------------------------------------------------
----------------------------------------------------------------

**TODAY'S AFFIRMATION:** All is well

**SPEND TIME WITH PEOPLE** WHO ARE GOOD FOR YOUR MENTAL HEALTH

# DAILY GRATITUDE

DATE ___ / ___ / ___

**TODAY I AM GRATEFUL FOR**

........................................................................................
........................................................................................
........................................................................................
........................................................................................
........................................................................................
........................................................................................
........................................................................................

**WHAT MADE ME FEEL HAPPY TODAY?**

~~~~~~~~~~~~~~~~~~~~~~~~~~~~~~~~~~~~~~~~~~~~~~~~~~~~~~~~~~~~~~~~~~~~~~~~~~~~~~~~~~~~~~~~
~~~~~~~~~~~~~~~~~~~~~~~~~~~~~~~~~~~~~~~~~~~~~~~~~~~~~~~~~~~~~~~~~~~~~~~~~~~~~~~~~~~~~~~~
~~~~~~~~~~~~~~~~~~~~~~~~~~~~~~~~~~~~~~~~~~~~~~~~~~~~~~~~~~~~~~~~~~~~~~~~~~~~~~~~~~~~~~~~

**THE ONE THING WHICH I AM MOST GRATEFUL FOR TODAY IS**

----------------------------------------------------------------------------------------
----------------------------------------------------------------------------------------

**TODAY'S AFFIRMATION:** I can do anything

# DAILY GRATITUDE

DATE ___ /___ /___

**TODAY I AM GRATEFUL FOR**

..........................................................
..........................................................
..........................................................
..........................................................
..........................................................
..........................................................
..........................................................

**WHAT MADE ME FEEL HAPPY TODAY?**

**THE ONE THING WHICH I AM MOST GRATEFUL FOR TODAY IS**

**TODAY'S AFFIRMATION:**

I make a difference

# DAILY GRATITUDE

DATE ___ / ___ / ___

**TODAY I AM GRATEFUL FOR**

..................................................................
..................................................................
..................................................................
..................................................................
..................................................................
..................................................................
..................................................................

**WHAT MADE ME FEEL HAPPY TODAY?**

**THE ONE THING WHICH I AM MOST GRATEFUL FOR TODAY IS**

-------------------------------------------------
-------------------------------------------------

**TODAY'S AFFIRMATION:** I am smart and strong

# DAILY GRATITUDE

DATE ___ / ___ / ___

**TODAY I AM GRATEFUL FOR**

........................................................................
........................................................................
........................................................................
........................................................................
........................................................................
........................................................................
........................................................................

**WHAT MADE ME FEEL HAPPY TODAY?**

~~~~~~~~~~~~~~~~~~~~~~~~~~~~~~~~~~~~~~~~~~~~~~~~~~~~~~
~~~~~~~~~~~~~~~~~~~~~~~~~~~~~~~~~~~~~~~~~~~~~~~~~~~~~~
~~~~~~~~~~~~~~~~~~~~~~~~~~~~~~~~~~~~~~~~~~~~~~~~~~~~~~

**THE ONE THING WHICH I AM MOST GRATEFUL FOR TODAY IS**

--------------------------------------------------------
--------------------------------------------------------

**TODAY'S AFFIRMATION:** *I love myself just as I am*

# DAILY GRATITUDE

DATE ___/___/___

### TODAY I AM GRATEFUL FOR

.................................................................
.................................................................
.................................................................
.................................................................
.................................................................
.................................................................

### WHAT MADE ME FEEL HAPPY TODAY?

~~~~~~~~~~~~~~~~~~~~~~~~~~~~~~~~~~~~~~~~~~~~~~~~~~~~~~~~~~~~~~~~~
~~~~~~~~~~~~~~~~~~~~~~~~~~~~~~~~~~~~~~~~~~~~~~~~~~~~~~~~~~~~~~~~~
~~~~~~~~~~~~~~~~~~~~~~~~~~~~~~~~~~~~~~~~~~~~~~~~~~~~~~~~~~~~~~~~~

### THE ONE THING WHICH I AM MOST GRATEFUL FOR TODAY IS

-----------------------------------------------------------------
-----------------------------------------------------------------

**TODAY'S AFFIRMATION:** *I easily achieve my goals*

# DAILY GRATITUDE

DATE ___ / ___ / ___

**TODAY I AM GRATEFUL FOR**

..................................................................
..................................................................
..................................................................
..................................................................
..................................................................
..................................................................
..................................................................

**WHAT MADE ME FEEL HAPPY TODAY?**

**THE ONE THING WHICH I AM MOST GRATEFUL FOR TODAY IS**

-------------------------------------------------------------------
-------------------------------------------------------------------

**TODAY'S AFFIRMATION:** I am **brave and courageous**

# DAILY GRATITUDE

DATE __ / __ / __

### TODAY I AM GRATEFUL FOR

..................................................................................
..................................................................................
..................................................................................
..................................................................................
..................................................................................
..................................................................................
..................................................................................

### WHAT MADE ME FEEL HAPPY TODAY?

~~~~~~~~~~~~~~~~~~~~~~~~~~~~~~~~~~~~~~~~~~~~~~~~~~~~~~~~~~~~~~~~~~~~~~~~~~~~~~~~~~
~~~~~~~~~~~~~~~~~~~~~~~~~~~~~~~~~~~~~~~~~~~~~~~~~~~~~~~~~~~~~~~~~~~~~~~~~~~~~~~~~~
~~~~~~~~~~~~~~~~~~~~~~~~~~~~~~~~~~~~~~~~~~~~~~~~~~~~~~~~~~~~~~~~~~~~~~~~~~~~~~~~~~

### THE ONE THING WHICH I AM MOST GRATEFUL FOR TODAY IS

----------------------------------------------------------------------------------
----------------------------------------------------------------------------------

**TODAY'S AFFIRMATION:** All is well

WE ARE ALL PERFECTLY *IMPERFECT*

# DAILY GRATITUDE

DATE ___ / ___ / ___

**TODAY I AM GRATEFUL FOR**

...........................................................................
...........................................................................
...........................................................................
...........................................................................
...........................................................................
...........................................................................

**WHAT MADE ME FEEL HAPPY TODAY?**

~~~~~~~~~~~~~~~~~~~~~~~~~~~~~~~~~~~~~~~~~~~~~~~~~~~~~~~~~~~~~~~~~~~~~~~~~~~
~~~~~~~~~~~~~~~~~~~~~~~~~~~~~~~~~~~~~~~~~~~~~~~~~~~~~~~~~~~~~~~~~~~~~~~~~~~
~~~~~~~~~~~~~~~~~~~~~~~~~~~~~~~~~~~~~~~~~~~~~~~~~~~~~~~~~~~~~~~~~~~~~~~~~~~

**THE ONE THING WHICH I AM MOST GRATEFUL FOR TODAY IS**

-----------------------------------------------------------------------
-----------------------------------------------------------------------

**TODAY'S AFFIRMATION:** I am enough

# DAILY GRATITUDE

DATE ___ /___ /___

**TODAY I AM GRATEFUL FOR**

.....................................................................................
.....................................................................................
.....................................................................................
.....................................................................................
.....................................................................................
.....................................................................................
.....................................................................................

**WHAT MADE ME FEEL HAPPY TODAY?**

**THE ONE THING WHICH I AM MOST GRATEFUL FOR TODAY IS**

**TODAY'S AFFIRMATION:**

**I am worthy**

# DAILY GRATITUDE

DATE ___ / ___ / ___

### TODAY I AM GRATEFUL FOR

..................................................................
..................................................................
..................................................................
..................................................................
..................................................................
..................................................................
..................................................................

### WHAT MADE ME FEEL HAPPY TODAY?

### THE ONE THING WHICH I AM MOST GRATEFUL FOR TODAY IS

------------------------------------------------------------------
------------------------------------------------------------------

**TODAY'S AFFIRMATION:**

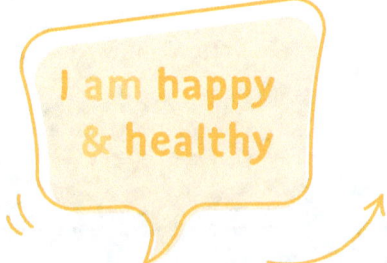

I am happy & healthy

# DAILY GRATITUDE

DATE ___ / ___ / ___

## TODAY I AM GRATEFUL FOR

..................................................................................................
..................................................................................................
..................................................................................................
..................................................................................................
..................................................................................................
..................................................................................................
..................................................................................................

## WHAT MADE ME FEEL HAPPY TODAY?

## THE ONE THING WHICH I AM MOST GRATEFUL FOR TODAY IS

**TODAY'S AFFIRMATION:** Everything is possible

# DAILY GRATITUDE

DATE ___/___/___

### TODAY I AM GRATEFUL FOR

........................................................................
........................................................................
........................................................................
........................................................................
........................................................................
........................................................................
........................................................................

### WHAT MADE ME FEEL HAPPY TODAY?

........................................................................
........................................................................
........................................................................

### THE ONE THING WHICH I AM MOST GRATEFUL FOR TODAY IS

------------------------------------------------------------------------
------------------------------------------------------------------------

**TODAY'S AFFIRMATION:** I am awesome

# DAILY GRATITUDE

DATE ___ / ___ / ___

**TODAY I AM GRATEFUL FOR**

..................................................................
..................................................................
..................................................................
..................................................................
..................................................................
..................................................................
..................................................................

**WHAT MADE ME FEEL HAPPY TODAY?**

~~~~~~~~~~~~~~~~~~~~~~~~~~~~~~~~~~~~~~~~~~~~~~~~~
~~~~~~~~~~~~~~~~~~~~~~~~~~~~~~~~~~~~~~~~~~~~~~~~~
~~~~~~~~~~~~~~~~~~~~~~~~~~~~~~~~~~~~~~~~~~~~~~~~~

**THE ONE THING WHICH I AM MOST GRATEFUL FOR TODAY IS**

------------------------------------------------------------
------------------------------------------------------------

**TODAY'S AFFIRMATION:**

**I am loved**

# DAILY GRATITUDE

DATE ___ /___ /___

### TODAY I AM GRATEFUL FOR

..................................................................................
..................................................................................
..................................................................................
..................................................................................
..................................................................................
..................................................................................
..................................................................................

### WHAT MADE ME FEEL HAPPY TODAY?

~~~~~~~~~~~~~~~~~~~~~~~~~~~~~~~~~~~~~~~~~~~~~~~~~~~~~~~~~~~~~~~~~~~~
~~~~~~~~~~~~~~~~~~~~~~~~~~~~~~~~~~~~~~~~~~~~~~~~~~~~~~~~~~~~~~~~~~~~
~~~~~~~~~~~~~~~~~~~~~~~~~~~~~~~~~~~~~~~~~~~~~~~~~~~~~~~~~~~~~~~~~~~~

### THE ONE THING WHICH I AM MOST GRATEFUL FOR TODAY IS

------------------------------------------------------------------
------------------------------------------------------------------

**TODAY'S AFFIRMATION:** *All is well*

IF YOU ARE
– HAPPY –
IF YOU ARE
FEELING GOOD
NOTHING ELSE
MATTERS

# CONGRATULATIONS

Simply fantastic! Well done! Congratulations on your 90 day gratitude and daily wins journey. Take a few minutes to review the following questions :

- Are you enjoying the process of writing down your appreciations and daily wins each day?
- Are you finding more things to be grateful for each day?
- Are you finding more daily wins and achievements?
- Are you feeling more positive emotions?
- Are you feeling less stressed?
- Are you feeling calmer?
- Are you feeling happier?
- Has your sleeping improved?
- Are you feeling healthier?
- Are you feeling more motivated?
- What other differences have you noticed?

# ...you have completed 90 days!

Completing 90 days is a fantastic achievement and I am proud of you for completing the journal. You have shown discipline, mindfulness and determination and should be proud of yourself for being a finisher. You have successfully created a positive daily habit which I hope you will continue.

Through your daily entries you've learned to appreciate the people and experiences that surround you, to count your blessings and ultimately cultivate a positive perspective on your life. This is just the beginning. Having an attitude of gratitude and celebrating your day-to-day achievements is a lifelong journey. So, grab yourself another journal, keep your momentum going, keep embracing the power of gratitude and it will continue to enrich your days with happiness, joy, fulfillment and positivity.

I wish for you daily well-being and a continued happy, abundant life.

For more information on well-being please visit www.simply-well-being.com

# DAILY WINS

DATE ___ /___ /___

**TODAY MY WINS WERE**

..................................................................................
..................................................................................
..................................................................................
..................................................................................
..................................................................................

**WELL-BEING:**    **PHYSICAL**    **MENTAL**    **SPIRITUAL**

/ 10      / 10      / 10

DATE ___ /___ /___

**TODAY MY WINS WERE**

..................................................................................
..................................................................................
..................................................................................
..................................................................................
..................................................................................

**WELL-BEING:**    **PHYSICAL**    **MENTAL**    **SPIRITUAL**

/ 10      / 10      / 10

DATE ___ /___ /___

**TODAY MY WINS WERE**

..................................................
..................................................
..................................................
..................................................
..................................................
..................................................
..................................................

WELL-BEING:

PHYSICAL    MENTAL    SPIRITUAL
  / 10        / 10       / 10

---

DATE ___ /___ /___

**TODAY MY WINS WERE**

..................................................
..................................................
..................................................
..................................................
..................................................

WELL-BEING:    PHYSICAL    MENTAL    SPIRITUAL
                 / 10        / 10       / 10

# DAILY WINS

DATE ___ / ___ / ___

**TODAY MY WINS WERE**

.................................................................................
.................................................................................
.................................................................................
.................................................................................
.................................................................................

WELL-BEING:   PHYSICAL   MENTAL   SPIRITUAL
              / 10       / 10     / 10

DATE ___ / ___ / ___

**TODAY MY WINS WERE**

.................................................................................
.................................................................................
.................................................................................
.................................................................................
.................................................................................

WELL-BEING:   PHYSICAL   MENTAL   SPIRITUAL
              / 10       / 10     / 10

DATE ___ /___ /___

**TODAY MY WINS WERE**

..................................................
..................................................
..................................................
..................................................
..................................................
..................................................
..................................................

WELL-BEING:

PHYSICAL   MENTAL   SPIRITUAL
  / 10       / 10      / 10

DATE ___ /___ /___

**TODAY MY WINS WERE**

..................................................
..................................................
..................................................
..................................................
..................................................

WELL-BEING:   PHYSICAL   MENTAL   SPIRITUAL
                / 10       / 10      / 10

# DAILY WINS

DATE ___ / ___ / ___

**TODAY MY WINS WERE**

........................................................................................................
........................................................................................................
........................................................................................................
........................................................................................................
........................................................................................................

WELL-BEING:   PHYSICAL     MENTAL      SPIRITUAL
                / 10         / 10         / 10

DATE ___ / ___ / ___

**TODAY MY WINS WERE**

........................................................................................................
........................................................................................................
........................................................................................................
........................................................................................................
........................................................................................................

WELL-BEING:   PHYSICAL     MENTAL      SPIRITUAL
                / 10         / 10         / 10

DATE ___ /___ /___

**TODAY MY WINS WERE**

........................................................
........................................................
........................................................
........................................................
........................................................
........................................................
........................................................

WELL-BEING:

PHYSICAL    MENTAL    SPIRITUAL
  / 10        / 10       / 10

---

DATE ___ /___ /___

**TODAY MY WINS WERE**

........................................................
........................................................
........................................................
........................................................
........................................................

WELL-BEING:    PHYSICAL    MENTAL    SPIRITUAL
                 / 10        / 10       / 10

# DAILY WINS

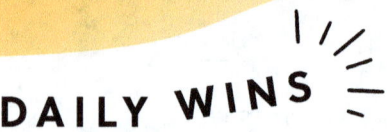

DATE ___/___/___

**TODAY MY WINS WERE**

........................................................................
........................................................................
........................................................................
........................................................................
........................................................................

WELL-BEING:   PHYSICAL   MENTAL   SPIRITUAL
                                / 10        / 10        / 10

---

DATE ___/___/___

**TODAY MY WINS WERE**

........................................................................
........................................................................
........................................................................
........................................................................
........................................................................

WELL-BEING:   PHYSICAL   MENTAL   SPIRITUAL
                                / 10        / 10        / 10

DATE ___ / ___ / ___

**TODAY MY WINS WERE**

........................................................
........................................................
........................................................
........................................................
........................................................
........................................................
........................................................

WELL-BEING:

PHYSICAL    MENTAL    SPIRITUAL
  / 10        / 10       / 10


DATE ___ / ___ / ___

**TODAY MY WINS WERE**

........................................................
........................................................
........................................................
........................................................
........................................................

WELL-BEING:    PHYSICAL    MENTAL    SPIRITUAL
                 / 10       / 10       / 10

# DAILY WINS

DATE ___ / ___ / ___

**TODAY MY WINS WERE**

..................................................................................................
..................................................................................................
..................................................................................................
..................................................................................................
..................................................................................................

WELL-BEING:   PHYSICAL   MENTAL   SPIRITUAL
                 / 10       / 10      / 10


DATE ___ / ___ / ___

**TODAY MY WINS WERE**

..................................................................................................
..................................................................................................
..................................................................................................
..................................................................................................
..................................................................................................

WELL-BEING:   PHYSICAL   MENTAL   SPIRITUAL
                 / 10       / 10      / 10

DATE ___ / ___ / ___

**TODAY MY WINS WERE**

........................................................

........................................................

........................................................

........................................................

........................................................

........................................................

........................................................

WELL-BEING:

PHYSICAL    MENTAL    SPIRITUAL

/ 10           / 10          / 10

DATE ___ / ___ / ___

**TODAY MY WINS WERE**

........................................................

........................................................

........................................................

........................................................

........................................................

WELL-BEING:    PHYSICAL    MENTAL    SPIRITUAL

/ 10           / 10          / 10

# DAILY WINS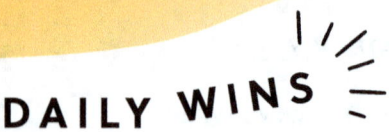

DATE ___ / ___ / ___

**TODAY MY WINS WERE**

...........................................................................................
...........................................................................................
...........................................................................................
...........................................................................................
...........................................................................................

WELL-BEING:   PHYSICAL   MENTAL   SPIRITUAL
                                / 10        / 10        / 10

DATE ___ / ___ / ___

**TODAY MY WINS WERE**

...........................................................................................
...........................................................................................
...........................................................................................
...........................................................................................
...........................................................................................

WELL-BEING:   PHYSICAL   MENTAL   SPIRITUAL
                                / 10        / 10        / 10

DATE ___ /___ /___

**TODY MY WINS WERE**

..............................................
..............................................
..............................................
..............................................
..............................................
..............................................
..............................................

WELL-BEING:

PHYSICAL    MENTAL    SPIRITUAL

/ 10      / 10      / 10

---

DATE ___ /___ /___

**TODAY MY WINS WERE**

..............................................
..............................................
..............................................
..............................................
..............................................

WELL-BEING:    PHYSICAL    MENTAL    SPIRITUAL

/ 10      / 10      / 10

# DAILY WINS

DATE ___ / ___ / ___

**TODAY MY WINS WERE**

..................................................................................
..................................................................................
..................................................................................
..................................................................................
..................................................................................

WELL-BEING:　　PHYSICAL　　MENTAL　　SPIRITUAL
　　　　　　　　　　/ 10　　　　 / 10　　　　 / 10

DATE ___ / ___ / ___

**TODAY MY WINS WERE**

..................................................................................
..................................................................................
..................................................................................
..................................................................................
..................................................................................

WELL-BEING:　　PHYSICAL　　MENTAL　　SPIRITUAL
　　　　　　　　　　/ 10　　　　 / 10　　　　 / 10

DATE ___/___/___

**TODAY MY WINS WERE**

.....................................................
.....................................................
.....................................................
.....................................................
.....................................................
.....................................................
.....................................................

WELL-BEING:

PHYSICAL   MENTAL   SPIRITUAL
/ 10           / 10          / 10

---

DATE ___/___/___

**TODAY MY WINS WERE**

.....................................................
.....................................................
.....................................................
.....................................................
.....................................................

WELL-BEING:   PHYSICAL   MENTAL   SPIRITUAL
/ 10           / 10          / 10

# DAILY WINS

DATE ___ /___ /___

**TODAY MY WINS WERE**

................................................................
................................................................
................................................................
................................................................
................................................................

WELL-BEING:   **PHYSICAL**   **MENTAL**   **SPIRITUAL**
                   / 10           / 10          / 10

DATE ___ /___ /___

**TODAY MY WINS WERE**

................................................................
................................................................
................................................................
................................................................
................................................................

WELL-BEING:   **PHYSICAL**   **MENTAL**   **SPIRITUAL**
                   / 10           / 10          / 10

DATE ___ /___ /___

**TODAY MY WINS WERE**

..................................................
..................................................
..................................................
..................................................
..................................................
..................................................
..................................................

WELL-BEING:

PHYSICAL    MENTAL    SPIRITUAL

/ 10        / 10        / 10

---

DATE ___ /___ /___

**TODAY MY WINS WERE**

..................................................
..................................................
..................................................
..................................................
..................................................

WELL-BEING:    PHYSICAL    MENTAL    SPIRITUAL

/ 10        / 10        / 10

## Random acts of kindness

Random acts of kindness are selfless gestures or actions that are given with no expectation of receiving anything in return. They bring joy and warmth to both the giver and receiver, spreading positivity and goodwill in the world.

They can be small gestures such as holding open a door for someone or helping someone carry their shopping to larger gestures such as buying someone lunch or helping with a community project.

Have you ever been the receiver of a random act of kindness? Have a think - what acts could you do this week for friends or strangers?

ONE KIND ACT
CAN CHANGE
SOMEONE'S
ENTIRE DAY

# DAILY WINS

DATE ___/___/___

**TODAY MY WINS WERE**

..................................................................................
..................................................................................
..................................................................................
..................................................................................
..................................................................................

WELL-BEING:   PHYSICAL   MENTAL   SPIRITUAL
              / 10       / 10     / 10

DATE ___/___/___

**TODAY MY WINS WERE**

..................................................................................
..................................................................................
..................................................................................
..................................................................................
..................................................................................

WELL-BEING:   PHYSICAL   MENTAL   SPIRITUAL
              / 10       / 10     / 10

DATE ___ /___ /___

**TODAY MY WINS WERE**

..................................................
..................................................
..................................................
..................................................
..................................................
..................................................
..................................................

WELL-BEING:

PHYSICAL   MENTAL   SPIRITUAL
  / 10      / 10      / 10

---

DATE ___ /___ /___

**TODAY MY WINS WERE**

..................................................................
..................................................................
..................................................................
..................................................................
..................................................................

WELL-BEING:   PHYSICAL   MENTAL   SPIRITUAL
                / 10      / 10      / 10

# DAILY WINS

DATE ___ / ___ / ___

**TODAY MY WINS WERE**

..................................................................................
..................................................................................
..................................................................................
..................................................................................
..................................................................................

WELL-BEING:   PHYSICAL     MENTAL     SPIRITUAL
                 / 10         / 10        / 10

DATE ___ / ___ / ___

**TODAY MY WINS WERE**

..................................................................................
..................................................................................
..................................................................................
..................................................................................
..................................................................................

WELL-BEING:   PHYSICAL     MENTAL     SPIRITUAL
                 / 10         / 10        / 10

DATE ___/___/___

**TODAY MY WINS WERE**

..................................................
..................................................
..................................................
..................................................
..................................................
..................................................
..................................................

WELL-BEING:

PHYSICAL    MENTAL    SPIRITUAL

/ 10      / 10      / 10

---

DATE ___/___/___

**TODAY MY WINS WERE**

..................................................
..................................................
..................................................
..................................................
..................................................

WELL-BEING:    PHYSICAL    MENTAL    SPIRITUAL

/ 10      / 10      / 10

# DAILY WINS

DATE ___/___/___

**TODAY MY WINS WERE**

..................................................................................
..................................................................................
..................................................................................
..................................................................................
..................................................................................

WELL-BEING:    **PHYSICAL**    **MENTAL**    **SPIRITUAL**
                       / 10         / 10         / 10

DATE ___/___/___

**TODAY MY WINS WERE**

..................................................................................
..................................................................................
..................................................................................
..................................................................................
..................................................................................

WELL-BEING:    **PHYSICAL**    **MENTAL**    **SPIRITUAL**
                       / 10         / 10         / 10

DATE ___ / ___ / ___

**TODAY MY WINS WERE**

...........................................................
...........................................................
...........................................................
...........................................................
...........................................................
...........................................................
...........................................................

WELL-BEING:

PHYSICAL   MENTAL   SPIRITUAL
  / 10       / 10       / 10

---

DATE ___ / ___ / ___

**TODAY MY WINS WERE**

...........................................................
...........................................................
...........................................................
...........................................................
...........................................................

WELL-BEING:   PHYSICAL   MENTAL   SPIRITUAL
                / 10       / 10       / 10

# DAILY WINS

DATE ___ / ___ / ___

**TODAY MY WINS WERE**

........................................................................
........................................................................
........................................................................
........................................................................
........................................................................

WELL-BEING:   PHYSICAL   MENTAL   SPIRITUAL
                 / 10      / 10      / 10

---

DATE ___ / ___ / ___

**TODAY MY WINS WERE**

........................................................................
........................................................................
........................................................................
........................................................................
........................................................................

WELL-BEING:   PHYSICAL   MENTAL   SPIRITUAL
                 / 10      / 10      / 10

DATE ___ / ___ / ___

**TODAY MY WINS WERE**

..................................................
..................................................
..................................................
..................................................
..................................................
..................................................
..................................................

WELL-BEING:

PHYSICAL    MENTAL    SPIRITUAL
  / 10         / 10       / 10

---

DATE ___ / ___ / ___

**TODAY MY WINS WERE**

..................................................
..................................................
..................................................
..................................................
..................................................

WELL-BEING:    PHYSICAL    MENTAL    SPIRITUAL
                 / 10        / 10       / 10

# DAILY WINS

DATE ___ / ___ / ___

**TODAY MY WINS WERE**

..................................................................................
..................................................................................
..................................................................................
..................................................................................
..................................................................................

WELL-BEING:   PHYSICAL   MENTAL   SPIRITUAL
              / 10       / 10     / 10

DATE ___ / ___ / ___

**TODAY MY WINS WERE**

..................................................................................
..................................................................................
..................................................................................
..................................................................................
..................................................................................

WELL-BEING:   PHYSICAL   MENTAL   SPIRITUAL
              / 10       / 10     / 10

DATE ___ /___ /___

**TODAY MY WINS WERE**

..................................................
..................................................
..................................................
..................................................
..................................................
..................................................
..................................................

**WELL-BEING:**

PHYSICAL   MENTAL   SPIRITUAL

/ 10             / 10            / 10

---

DATE ___ /___ /___

**TODAY MY WINS WERE**

..................................................
..................................................
..................................................
..................................................
..................................................

**WELL-BEING:**   PHYSICAL   MENTAL   SPIRITUAL

/ 10             / 10            / 10

# DAILY WINS

DATE ___/___/___

**TODAY MY WINS WERE**

..................................................................
..................................................................
..................................................................
..................................................................
..................................................................

WELL-BEING:    PHYSICAL    MENTAL    SPIRITUAL
                                / 10        / 10        / 10

DATE ___/___/___

**TODAY MY WINS WERE**

..................................................................
..................................................................
..................................................................
..................................................................
..................................................................

WELL-BEING:    PHYSICAL    MENTAL    SPIRITUAL
                                / 10        / 10        / 10

DATE ___ /___ /___

**TODAY MY WINS WERE**

..........................................

..............................................................

................................................................

....................................................................

.................................................................

............................................................

.........................................................

WELL-BEING:

PHYSICAL    MENTAL    SPIRITUAL
  / 10          / 10         / 10

---

DATE ___ /___ /___

**TODAY MY WINS WERE**

................................................................................

................................................................................

................................................................................

................................................................................

................................................................................

WELL-BEING:    PHYSICAL    MENTAL    SPIRITUAL
                  / 10          / 10         / 10

# DAILY WINS

DATE ___/___/___

**TODAY MY WINS WERE**

..................................................
..................................................
..................................................
..................................................
..................................................

WELL-BEING:  PHYSICAL   MENTAL   SPIRITUAL
             / 10       / 10     / 10

DATE ___/___/___

**TODAY MY WINS WERE**

..................................................
..................................................
..................................................
..................................................
..................................................

WELL-BEING:  PHYSICAL   MENTAL   SPIRITUAL
             / 10       / 10     / 10

DATE ___ / ___ / ___

**TODAY MY WINS WERE**

..................................................
..................................................
..................................................
..................................................
..................................................
..................................................
..................................................

WELL-BEING:

PHYSICAL    MENTAL    SPIRITUAL
  / 10       / 10       / 10

DATE ___ / ___ / ___

**TODAY MY WINS WERE**

..................................................
..................................................
..................................................
..................................................
..................................................

WELL-BEING:   PHYSICAL    MENTAL    SPIRITUAL
                / 10       / 10       / 10

## Positive Affirmations

Positive affirmations are positive statements which you can repeat to yourself to help shift negative thoughts or beliefs to more positive uplifting ones. By repeating positive affirmations over time, they can boost your self-esteem, self-confidence and overall well-being.

There are a few rules to remember when writing your own positive affirmations:

1. Affirmations should be positive – avoid negatives.
2. Always use the present tense – as if the statement is already true.
3. Focus on the solution and not the problem.
4. Keep them specific, short and simple – so that you can easily remember them.

Write yourself three positive affirmations or take three which you like from the gratitude pages in this journal and repeat them three times a day to yourself for 30 days.

A POSITIVE DAY *BEGINS WITH* A POSITIVE MINDSET

# DAILY WINS

DATE ___ / ___ / ___

**TODAY MY WINS WERE**

..................................................................................
..................................................................................
..................................................................................
..................................................................................
..................................................................................

WELL-BEING:   PHYSICAL   MENTAL   SPIRITUAL
                  / 10       / 10       / 10

DATE ___ / ___ / ___

**TODAY MY WINS WERE**

..................................................................................
..................................................................................
..................................................................................
..................................................................................
..................................................................................

WELL-BEING:   PHYSICAL   MENTAL   SPIRITUAL
                  / 10       / 10       / 10

DATE ___ /___ /___

**TODAY MY WINS WERE**

..................................................
..................................................
..................................................
..................................................
..................................................
..................................................
..................................................

WELL-BEING:

PHYSICAL    MENTAL    SPIRITUAL
 / 10         / 10        / 10

---

DATE ___ /___ /___

**TODAY MY WINS WERE**

..................................................
..................................................
..................................................
..................................................
..................................................

WELL-BEING:    PHYSICAL    MENTAL    SPIRITUAL
                 / 10        / 10        / 10

# DAILY WINS

DATE ___ / ___ / ___

**TODAY MY WINS WERE**

..................................................................................
..................................................................................
..................................................................................
..................................................................................
..................................................................................

WELL-BEING:   PHYSICAL    MENTAL    SPIRITUAL
              / 10        / 10      / 10

DATE ___ / ___ / ___

**TODAY MY WINS WERE**

..................................................................................
..................................................................................
..................................................................................
..................................................................................
..................................................................................

WELL-BEING:   PHYSICAL    MENTAL    SPIRITUAL
              / 10        / 10      / 10

DATE ___ /___ /___

**TODAY MY WINS WERE**

..................................................
..................................................
..................................................
..................................................
..................................................
..................................................
..................................................

WELL-BEING:

PHYSICAL / 10   MENTAL / 10   SPIRITUAL / 10

---

DATE ___ /___ /___

**TODAY MY WINS WERE**

..................................................
..................................................
..................................................
..................................................
..................................................

WELL-BEING:   PHYSICAL / 10   MENTAL / 10   SPIRITUAL / 10

# DAILY WINS

DATE ___/___/___

**TODAY MY WINS WERE**

..................................................................
..................................................................
..................................................................
..................................................................
..................................................................

WELL-BEING:  PHYSICAL    MENTAL    SPIRITUAL
             / 10         / 10      / 10

---

DATE ___/___/___

**TODAY MY WINS WERE**

..................................................................
..................................................................
..................................................................
..................................................................
..................................................................

WELL-BEING:  PHYSICAL    MENTAL    SPIRITUAL
             / 10         / 10      / 10

DATE ___ /___ /___

**TODAY MY WINS WERE**

..................................................
..................................................
..................................................
..................................................
..................................................
..................................................
..................................................

WELL-BEING:
PHYSICAL    MENTAL    SPIRITUAL
  / 10       / 10       / 10

---

DATE ___ /___ /___

**TODAY MY WINS WERE**

..................................................
..................................................
..................................................
..................................................
..................................................

WELL-BEING:   PHYSICAL    MENTAL    SPIRITUAL
                / 10       / 10       / 10

# DAILY WINS

DATE ___/___/___

**TODAY MY WINS WERE**

........................................................................................
........................................................................................
........................................................................................
........................................................................................
........................................................................................

WELL-BEING:  PHYSICAL   MENTAL   SPIRITUAL
                / 10      / 10      / 10


DATE ___/___/___

**TODAY MY WINS WERE**

........................................................................................
........................................................................................
........................................................................................
........................................................................................
........................................................................................

WELL-BEING:  PHYSICAL   MENTAL   SPIRITUAL
                / 10      / 10      / 10

DATE ___ /___ /___

**TODAY MY WINS WERE**

........................................
..........................................
............................................
..............................................
................................................
..................................................
....................................................

WELL-BEING:

PHYSICAL    MENTAL    SPIRITUAL
  / 10        / 10       / 10

---

DATE ___ /___ /___

**TODAY MY WINS WERE**

....................................................
....................................................
....................................................
....................................................
....................................................

WELL-BEING:   PHYSICAL    MENTAL    SPIRITUAL
                / 10        / 10       / 10

# DAILY WINS

DATE ___/___/___

**TODAY MY WINS WERE**

..................................................................................
..................................................................................
..................................................................................
..................................................................................
..................................................................................

WELL-BEING:   **PHYSICAL**   **MENTAL**   **SPIRITUAL**
                  / 10           / 10          / 10

DATE ___/___/___

**TODAY MY WINS WERE**

..................................................................................
..................................................................................
..................................................................................
..................................................................................
..................................................................................

WELL-BEING:   **PHYSICAL**   **MENTAL**   **SPIRITUAL**
                  / 10           / 10          / 10

DATE ___ / ___ / ___

**TODAY MY WINS WERE**

..................................................
..................................................
..................................................
..................................................
..................................................
..................................................
..................................................

WELL-BEING:

PHYSICAL    MENTAL    SPIRITUAL

/ 10          / 10        / 10

---

DATE ___ / ___ / ___

**TODAY MY WINS WERE**

..................................................
..................................................
..................................................
..................................................
..................................................

WELL-BEING:    PHYSICAL    MENTAL    SPIRITUAL

/ 10          / 10        / 10

# DAILY WINS

DATE ___/___/___

**TODAY MY WINS WERE**

..................................................................................
..................................................................................
..................................................................................
..................................................................................
..................................................................................

WELL-BEING:   PHYSICAL   MENTAL   SPIRITUAL
                 / 10         / 10       / 10

DATE ___/___/___

**TODAY MY WINS WERE**

..................................................................................
..................................................................................
..................................................................................
..................................................................................
..................................................................................

WELL-BEING:   PHYSICAL   MENTAL   SPIRITUAL
                 / 10         / 10       / 10

DATE ___ /___ /___

**TODAY MY WINS WERE**

..........................................
..........................................
..........................................
..........................................
..........................................
..........................................
..........................................

WELL-BEING:
PHYSICAL   MENTAL   SPIRITUAL
  / 10       / 10      / 10


DATE ___ /___ /___

**TODAY MY WINS WERE**

..........................................
..........................................
..........................................
..........................................
..........................................

WELL-BEING:   PHYSICAL   MENTAL   SPIRITUAL
                / 10       / 10      / 10

# DAILY WINS

DATE ___/___/___

**TODAY MY WINS WERE**

..................................................................................
..................................................................................
..................................................................................
..................................................................................
..................................................................................

WELL-BEING:   PHYSICAL    MENTAL    SPIRITUAL
              / 10         / 10      / 10

DATE ___/___/___

**TODAY MY WINS WERE**

..................................................................................
..................................................................................
..................................................................................
..................................................................................
..................................................................................

WELL-BEING:   PHYSICAL    MENTAL    SPIRITUAL
              / 10         / 10      / 10

DATE ___/___/___

**TODAY MY WINS WERE**

......................................................
......................................................
......................................................
......................................................
......................................................
......................................................
......................................................

WELL-BEING:

PHYSICAL  MENTAL  SPIRITUAL

/ 10       / 10     / 10

---

DATE ___/___/___

**TODAY MY WINS WERE**

......................................................
......................................................
......................................................
......................................................
......................................................

WELL-BEING:   PHYSICAL   MENTAL   SPIRITUAL

/ 10       / 10     / 10

# DAILY WINS

DATE ___ / ___ / ___

**TODAY MY WINS WERE**

............................................................
............................................................
............................................................
............................................................
............................................................

WELL-BEING:   **PHYSICAL**   **MENTAL**   **SPIRITUAL**
                  / 10            / 10          / 10

DATE ___ / ___ / ___

**TODAY MY WINS WERE**

............................................................
............................................................
............................................................
............................................................
............................................................

WELL-BEING:   **PHYSICAL**   **MENTAL**   **SPIRITUAL**
                  / 10            / 10          / 10

DATE ___ /___ /___

**TODAY MY WINS WERE**

..................................................
..................................................
..................................................
..................................................
..................................................
..................................................
..................................................

WELL-BEING:

PHYSICAL   MENTAL   SPIRITUAL

/ 10           / 10           / 10

---

DATE ___ /___ /___

**TODAY MY WINS WERE**

..................................................
..................................................
..................................................
..................................................
..................................................

WELL-BEING:   PHYSICAL   MENTAL   SPIRITUAL

/ 10           / 10           / 10

# Daily Wins Journal

**CELEBRATE YOUR
DAILY SUCCESSES**
NO MATTER HOW SMALL

# JUST TAKE
## THE NEXT STEP

# Acknowledgements

I love it when you awake one morning and receive the inspiration to pursue a really fun project. That is what this journal has been for me and I am grateful to have had the time and resource to be able to bring it to life.

I would like to thank my children, Haydn and Amanie, for their help and ideas. I wanted this journal to appeal to a younger generation than myself and therefore their guidance was invaluable. Thank you to my Mum who has helped me to edit this journal and to Silke Spingies my fantastic designer who has helped to bring my vision to life.

And finally to you the journaler, thank you for choosing my journal.

# About the Author

Mary Parrish is from the UK and, at the time of writing this book, lives in Switzerland with her husband and two children. She spent over 20 years of her life in Corporate Marketing and Project roles as well as training in alternative therapies in her spare time. She was able to pursue her love of well-being after the move to Switzerland when she finally had time to put pen to paper. She is currently a business and well-being coach.

## Qualifications

Hypnotherapist

Spiritual Response Therapist

Reiki Healer

Energy Healer

Indian Head Massage Therapist

HypnoBirthing Practitioner

www.simply-well-being.com

www.ingramcontent.com/pod-product-compliance
Lightning Source LLC
Chambersburg PA
CBHW071452080526
44587CB00014B/2076